"*How Can I Help?* is an invaluable resource for seminary students, laypersons, church staff and pastors who truly want to impact the lives of others."

Dr. Tony Evans, senior pastor,
Oak Cliff Bible Fellowship, Dallas, Texas;
president, The Urban Alternative

"I interview people every day who stand face-to-face with the suffering in our world. Many people earnestly desire to help but do not know how because they lack information. This book teaches people how to help, how to listen and how to respond confidently in specific areas when trouble comes. Lynda's insights are powerful; she is truly the expert helper. Her book is a must for everyone."

Terry Meeuwsen, cohost, The 700 Club

"When you are confronted with someone in trouble, whether it is a relative, friend or stranger, you need tools to help them in the most effective way possible. Lynda Elliott's book offers incredibly practical helps for anyone called on to help a person in emotional, physical or spiritual pain. In nonthreatening layman's terms, Elliott offers tools and insights that will enable the most timid helper to offer assistance that can make a difference."

Jan Silvious, Women of Faith, author, broadcaster

"*How Can I Help?* is a practical and insightful guide for every pastor, counselor and layperson ministering to others. Full of examples and scriptural reinforcements, the sections helping those experiencing anger, depression, fear, temptation and betrayal will be a welcome addition to every resource library. Packed with wise suggestions from a licensed professional, this book is a blueprint for caregivers working in bereavement counseling and with physical and emotional illnesses."

Norma Dearing, broadcaster and author of
The Healing Touch

"*How Can I Help?* answers the questions everyone needs at some time in life. I cannot think of a situation that this book does not cover. It is not only easy to read, but it is an at-your-fingertips resource for everyone who reads it. It is a classic book of wisdom and hope."

Sandy Smith, Bailey Smith Ministries

"Lynda Elliott is an exceptionally wise and gifted helper, teacher and speaker. In her classes at Trinity, I have witnessed the dramatic impact she has on others as she teaches them to recognize their own uniqueness as well as their abilities to help others."

Pamela Peterson, Ph.D., Dean of Women's Studies,
Trinity College and Seminary, Newburgh, Indiana

"This book is a must-read. We all experience difficulties in life, and we need to learn how to help one another effectively. Lynda Elliott packs more concrete, usable instruction in one chapter than is available in most books. Compiling thirty year's experience, she addresses specific areas of difficulty and teaches helpers how to maintain personal balance while becoming involved in the life of another person. This book is also an excellent resource for discussion in groups of any size."

Mamie McCullough, speaker, author

"Lynda's book is a tremendous resource for helping the people when trouble enters their lives. It offers practical, hands-on methods. Everyone should have a copy of this book. I heartily recommend it!"

Linda Strom, Discipleship Unlimited, author of
Karla Faye Tucker Set Free

HOW CAN I
HELP?

How Can I Help?

*Caring for People
without Harming Them or Yourself*

Lynda D. Elliott

Chosen Books

A Division of Baker Book House Co
Grand Rapids, Michigan 49516

© 2003 by Lynda D. Elliott

Published by Chosen Books
A division of Baker Book House Company
P.O. Box 6287, Grand Rapids, MI 49516-6287
www.bakerbooks.com

Second printing, September 2003

Printed in the United States of America

Library of Congress Cataloging-in-Publication Data

Elliott, Lynda D.
    How can I help? : caring for people without harming them or yourself / Lynda D. Elliott.
        p.   cm.
    Includes bibliographical references.
    ISBN 0-8007-9315-3 (pbk.)
    1. Helping behavior—Religious aspects—Christianity. I. Title.
BV4647.H4 E44 2003
241′.677—dc21   2002151971

This book is dedicated to my precious grandchildren,
Seth, Sawyer, Kristina and Brian.

I thank God for each one of you.
What a gift you are to me!
I pray that God will always bless you
with good friends.
Always remember that your best friend is Jesus.

CONTENTS

ACKNOWLEDGMENTS

Nobody ever really gets anything done alone. I have many people to thank for helping me with this book. First, I want to thank the people who have so graciously shared their lives with me. Other than God's Word, they have been my primary teachers.

My husband, Wayne, has been his usual supportive, constant self. He has helped me in many ways, such as cooking meals, taking care of computer problems when I can't unscramble my messes, and just encouraging me to keep writing. He has been the best friend a wife and writer could wish for!

Everybody needs cheerleaders, and I have a great team. I want to say thank you to Carolyn Johnson, Sandy Smith, Jan Silvious, Melissa Clark, Lynda Sorrells, Jane Anne Smith, Stacey Pitts, Bill Smith, Nancy Grisham, Judy Martin, Carolyn Russell, Jetta Allen, and Carole Harvey. All of you have helped at critical times when I have needed encouragement and a helping hand. Without a doubt, I would not have completed this book without you.

My editors, Jane Campbell and Ann Weinheimer . . . I call you the world's best editors! Not only are you capable, but you are fun, patient and open to discussion. With you, it's a smooth trip!

ONE

COMMON QUESTIONS ABOUT HELPING

Trouble comes. Jesus told us it would come: "In the world you have tribulation and trials and distress and frustration" (John 16:33). We do not like to think about it, but whether we think about trouble or not, it comes.

You may have a friend who is seriously ill. Your best friend may have an affair. Family members may have a disagreement and stop speaking to each other. The child of a friend may die. You may have a neighbor who is abusing her child. A tornado or flood or hurricane may come and destroy homes and lives. We do not like trouble, but when it comes, people in our families, neighborhoods, offices, churches and maybe even strangers could need our help.

When people turn to you for help, do you believe that you usually know what to say or do? Are you afraid that you will say or do the wrong thing and do more harm than good? *Would you like to know how to help people without harming them or yourself?*

As a professional counselor, I provided help for people in trouble for more than 25 years. Each week people came to my office and began by saying, "I really need to talk to someone." As they poured out their life stories, their relief soon became evident. Even before problem solving began, their tightly gripped, twisting hands began to relax. They took a deep breath. They were in a safe place. The weight of their burdens was being shared by someone who listened. Hope began.

> Have you experienced the relief that comes from sharing your burden with another person who cares? Who was that person? What were your circumstances?

Near the end of our sessions, I usually asked, "Do you have a close friend or family member?" Recently I received this revealing response to that question: "Yes, I have, but they don't know what to do. They sent me here. I guess getting a counselor is sort of like buying a fake friend or family member who understands and knows what to say."

Although professional counselors are indispensable, I believe that no one should have to "buy" help that a friend or family member can become equipped to give. As believers, we need to know how to enter into crises with those we love and minister effectively.

In fact, with a client's permission, I often asked a supportive friend or family member to be available to the client between counseling sessions. At first they all had similar questions:

> "Who am I to help anyone? I've made too many mistakes in my own life!"

> "What if I say or do the wrong thing? What if I hurt instead of help?"

16

"What if I don't know what to say?"

"What if have not had the same type of problem? And what if I have?"

"How can I keep from giving too much?"

"How can I protect my time?"

"How can I keep the person from becoming too dependent on me?"

"How can I be honest without offending?"

"What if I have to break a promise?"

"What about lending money?"

"How will I know if the person needs professional help? If so, what then?"

Have you ever needed answers to any of these questions? If so, which ones concern you the most?

These are all valid questions, and answers are needed. In this chapter I will offer answers to each of these questions, but first I want to tell you about one of the simplest, most powerful gifts you can give.

> *Do you often find yourself asking, "What can I do?" What services are you thinking about providing?*

Your Most Valuable Contribution

As you can see, most of the above questions are about *doing.* We always ask, "What can I *do* to help?" And this is important. But we need to recognize that just committing to *be with* someone through a period of difficulty is the most valuable contribution we will ever make.

When Jesus was in the Garden of Gethsemane, one of His primary needs was for the company of His disciples. Matthew 26:37–38 says:

And taking with Him Peter and the two sons of Zebedee, He began to show grief and distress of mind and was deeply depressed. Then He said to them, My soul is very sad and deeply grieved, so that I am almost dying of sorrow. Stay here and keep awake and watch with Me.

Jesus began to pray again and when He returned to His disciples, they were asleep. He said to them, "Are you so utterly unable to stay awake and watch with Me for one hour?" (Matthew 26:40). Jesus asked His friends to be with Him in prayer three times, and each time His friends went to sleep instead.

Jesus did not need His disciples to *do* anything for Him because He had already surrendered to the will of His Father and knew that the time of death was approaching. Their presence was not only what He desired the *most,* it was *all* He needed. Your presence in someone's life is a valuable gift that can make all the difference. Why is that true? *I believe that it is true because your presence is a visible image of the invisible presence of the Holy Spirit.*

Have you ever felt totally alone? What did you need that you did not have?

For example, a friend named Jill told me this story. "Last spring my mother died. Her death introduced me to a level of grief that I had never imagined. I felt as if the ground were shifting right under my feet. I had been so close to my mother and I could not believe that she was gone. After her death, many people came to our house. Many kind words were spoken, but I cannot remember anything that was said. I guess I was in shock, but I *do* remember my friend Jane.

"Jane worked in our kitchen, making and serving coffee to our guests. When she was not working, she simply sat quietly in the blue chair in our living room. When grief would overwhelm me and life would feel unreal, the quiet, familiar presence of my friend settled me. I knew she understood that I just needed her to be there in the room so that I could find her when the next wave of grief rolled over me."

Can you recall a time when someone's presence was enough? If so, what were the circumstances? What did his or her presence do for you?

Although we do need to learn how to respond in specific, helpful ways, the most important thing in the life of a hurting person is *our presence*. That is the bedrock of effective helping. Just like Jesus, we need someone who truly cares about us when we are suffering. When God provided the Body of Christ, He made that kind of loving care possible.

Several years ago, I had spine surgery. For the first 24 hours after surgery, I slept most of the time. Nurses and other medical personnel were available to me at any moment, but during those first few hours I did not want to be left alone. Whenever I woke for a few moments, I saw my husband, Wayne, sitting by the bed. Just knowing he was there gave me comfort and a feeling of safety.

Questions You May Have

Now let us return to the questions that people ask when they are called to help. You might want to record your thoughts and ideas in a notebook for handy reference.

"Who am I to help anyone? I've made too many mistakes in my own life!"

Because of sins in your past, you may believe that you are truly not fit to help anyone. If, however, you have gained wisdom from your past experiences, your mistakes can become excellent teaching tools.

Proverbs 5:1–2 tells us the value of wisdom. It enables us to "exercise proper discrimination and discretion." Many people commit sins and make serious mistakes and learn absolutely nothing, but if you have let God teach and change you, you can be a valuable helper.

Some of the most effective helpers are those who have learned from past mistakes. They have emerged from failure with treasures of wisdom in their grasp.

Have you let past sins disqualify you as a helper? If you look back, can you define lessons that you learned from your experiences? Can you see how the lessons you learned could help someone else? What were some of those experiences? Can you agree that if you have gained wisdom, your past is not a liability; it has become an asset?

A man named Charles told me the following: "I had begun meeting a woman from my athletic club after work. I thought we would just be able to talk and be friends, but before long I was contemplating an affair. I have played golf with three friends for several years, but I began skipping our golf afternoons and meeting this woman instead. One day a man named George, who was in our foursome, called me and asked me to meet him for an early breakfast the next morning.

"The next morning as I lifted my coffee cup to my mouth, George said, 'Charles, I have a hunch that you're about to get into some real trouble. Are you thinking about having an affair?'

"I know my eyes just about popped out over the rim of my cup! I have never been so surprised, or so embarrassed. I tried to avoid giving a direct answer by asking George why he thought I might be involved with someone.

"George told me that he had had an affair several years before and, because of that, he recognized the signs. He commented on my new clothes, my updated haircut, and the fact that I was working out and losing weight. He added the fact that I was no longer available to play golf, which was a big change for me.

"When I admitted my feelings to him, George told me how difficult having an affair can be, describing the complexity of covering up, lying and justifying the changes in my schedule and behavior. He told me that he had been praying for me because he knew that I would soon be experiencing guilt and shame if I did not change directions. He cautioned me about the possibility of disappointing and losing my family. While we were talking, I realized how preoccupied I had become. My sinful thoughts had caused me to have tunnel vision. In my pursuit of another woman, I had lost sight of everyone who was most important to me. I broke off the relationship that night. I will always be grateful that God used George's sin to rescue me from disaster."

"What if I say or do the wrong thing? What if I hurt instead of help?"

There will be times when you say or do the wrong thing because you are not a perfect person! Although we are all responsible to become equipped to help, no matter how much we learn, we will still make some mistakes. Our Father knows this and He will pour out grace on us when we do.

When you make a mistake, the first step is to face it and admit it to yourself. Tell God about it and if He leads, apologize to the one you hurt. Do it immediately. Acknowledging your mistake will help you to stay humble. Then be sure to grow in knowledge so that you do not make the same mistake again.

Remember: Your error is not what will make the difference; however, your humility and desire to make things right will teach a life lesson.

For example, Joan befriended a woman named Margaret who recently joined her book club. Margaret was seriously overweight and had recently been diagnosed with high blood pressure and heart disease. They discussed the importance of losing weight, but Margaret was not highly motivated to begin that task. Joan is a very enthusiastic person who values physical fitness. When they met again, Joan brought Margaret a membership application to her health club, which offered an exercise and diet program.

Has someone ever given you advice or suggestions prematurely or imposed values on you? If so, how did you feel?

Joan had expected Margaret to appreciate the efforts she had made to get her on the right track toward good health, so she was stunned when Margaret said, "When I decide to lose weight, I'll make my own arrangements."

Although Joan meant well, she had offended Margaret. She did not realize that just because fitness was important to her, it was not equally important to Margaret. Margaret felt "managed" and did not want to be pushed into good health.

Joan had assumed that Margaret would feel as *she* did and do what *she* would have done. Her assumptions were false. When she realized what she had done, she apologized for imposing her own values on Margaret. She made a mistake, admitted it and Margaret forgave her. A few weeks later, Margaret asked Joan for the form to apply for membership to the fitness club and began to take her health seriously.

"What if I don't know what to say?"

There may be times when you are completely stumped. Just be honest about that. It is a good time for your friend to realize that her helper does not know everything!

Now think about what you usually do when you are stumped. Don't you pray and study God's Word? Don't you obey the leading of the Holy Spirit? Doesn't He usually lead you one step at a time? If you know how to follow Him in your own life, just continue the same process with your friend in her life.

If you find that you lack information about a specific issue, do some research. Books are available on almost every topic. You can also obtain information from the Internet. Knowledge is the basis for wise actions, so get the facts that you need. If you teach your friend how to search for truth from Scripture and teach her how to find

> *How many sources of knowledge can you identify? Which ones are available to you?*

information from additional resources, she will be able to make her own search in the future.

Cathie learned the value of study and research when she found that her neighbor Polly, a single mother with three children, had been diagnosed with multiple sclerosis.

Polly was anxious about an appointment with a specialist and she knew almost nothing about her condition. She asked Cathie many questions: "Did God send this sickness to me? Am I being punished for something?

Is there any treatment? Have you ever heard of anyone who had MS who got well? Will I be able to take care of my children?"

Although Cathie knew nothing about multiple sclerosis, she did know Scripture and she knew how to pray. Cathie taught Polly how to use a concordance so that she could study Scriptures about healing, and they began to pray together for guidance and healing.

Cathie was also a computer expert, so she taught Polly how to look for medical information on the Internet. Together they found numerous articles that gave Polly helpful information regarding her condition, enabling her to ask important questions when she met her new physician.

Do you believe that practical help can be as useful as "spiritual" help? Why or why not? When you have provided practical help, have you felt that your help was not as "spiritual" as it should have been?

Because of Cathie's willingness to help, Polly developed skills that benefited her as long as she needed treatment. Step by step through prayer and study, Cathie and Polly worked their way through a maze of problems and found solutions. They found help with childcare, lined up temporary help with housework, and worked out transportation to and from Polly's initial treatment. Within a few months, Polly was able to return to her position as a high school teacher.

"What if I have not had the same type of problem? And what if I have?"

You will probably encounter people who have suffered in ways that you have not. If that is the case, remember that although your circumstances may have been different, most of us initially respond to trouble in the same way. For instance, have we not all experienced the pain of grief? Have we not all faced sickness in some form? Do we not know what it is to feel fearful at times? Angry? Bitter? When we enter periods of difficulty, most of us experience intense emotional responses. These feelings are universal. *If you cannot identify with a particular problem, identify with the feeling that someone is expressing.*

When Tom, a successful banker, related the story of his divorce, I said, "I haven't been divorced, but I understand grief. I know how hard it is to lose someone you love. I lost my father during my first year of college." That was all Tom needed to hear to feel that I understood his pain.

If, on the other hand, someone shares a problem that you have faced, be sure that you have received sufficient healing and have grown to the place where you can help. If not, you may find yourself over-identifying with the person who is experiencing the same circumstances that previously harmed you. You may become anxious as your own memories begin to surface.

A friend named Donna shared this with me: "I was diagnosed with breast cancer three years ago. I have been cancer-free for two years, but I still become very anxious when I go for my checkups. Recently a woman in our neighborhood was diagnosed with breast cancer. I wanted to go right over and encourage her, but I just couldn't make myself go. I wasn't ready to talk with someone who had cancer, so I finally just sent a card. Obviously, I needed more time and distance from my own experience."

It was obvious to Donna that her emotions were not as recovered as her body. As time passes, perhaps she will be more and more able to help someone in that situation, but that was not the time.

There are seasons in our lives. If you know that you are not ready to serve in a particular area, give yourself the freedom to wait. Timing is very important. God is not necessarily calling you to help just because you care. Pray and proceed carefully before you force yourself to go beyond the boundaries of your well being.

"How can I keep from giving too much?"

John's best friend, Robert, lost his job when his company downsized. Not long after losing his job, Robert was in a car wreck. When he got out of the hospital, he was instructed to be in physical therapy for three months before attempting to return to work. John offered to meet with Robert once a week for a Bible study, hoping to be an encouragement to him about his health and future employment.

What are the most intense feelings that you have experienced in your life? Do people around you appear to be experiencing the same feelings? Are there areas where you believe that you are not ready to help? If so, what are they? Will you ask God if He is calling you to grow in those areas?

Three weeks later, John said, "I don't know what I'm going to do about Robert. He calls several times a day even when I'm at work. Within an hour after I get home, he calls again. I know he's miserable and bored, and I want to be a good friend during this time, but I feel as if he's taking over my life! I don't want to hurt him, but I feel pressured and drained. I can't give any more!"

Although it may sound noble to help someone until we are exhausted, it is not. Our judgment is not good when we are overtired and our patience can wear thin during times of stress. Few crises are so serious that it becomes necessary for us to wear ourselves out. We need to develop realistic expectations of ourselves and teach others to do the same.

For example, years ago I worked in the area of child abuse. I trained lay counselors to go into the homes of parents who were abusing their children and help rehabilitate them. Because the lives of small, helpless children were at stake, my work was very stressful. During my first year in that position, I gave it everything I had, telling myself that it was the least I could do.

Have you ever worn yourself out, believing that you were doing a good thing? Have you given more than you had to give? Did your friends or family complain about being neglected? Were their complaints justified? What would you like to do differently next time?

At the end of that first year, my supervisor pointed out that my dedication to exhaustion was not admirable. He told me that some of the decisions I had made when I was fatigued were not of the best quality, and he feared I had begun to neglect my family. Because I had used none of my vacation days the past year, he instructed me to take two days off each month. He informed me that if he called my office and found me there during those two days, he would put me on probation! What a shock it was to me to realize that I had not been noble and self-sacrificing but simply overworked and foolish!

You cannot continue to help people unless you become willing to find rest for yourself and take care of your own needs. It may help you to do this if you encourage the person you are helping to seek assistance from additional people.

27

If you are going to stay fit to serve, you must take responsibility for finding balance in your own life. When you do, you will also be setting a good example for the one you are helping.

"How can I protect my time?"

People who are suffering often forget that others have lives of their own. All they know is that they need help. For example, if you have an earache, what are you thinking about all the time? That is the way hurting people are. More than anything, they are looking for ways to get out of pain. If you are not careful, their lives can consume your every waking moment.

Just as you need to protect yourself from becoming drained emotionally, as we saw in the previous section, so you need to protect your available time. Think about your family and remember the people God has already placed in your life. Consider your responsibilities at home and at work. When you become involved in a season of helping, let your friend know when you can be available and when you cannot. Give information about your life early in the crisis. When you set limits early, your friend will be able to form a picture of your life and his place in it. If you fail to do this, the person you are helping may feel rejected when you have to set time limits.

For example, you might say, "I will be happy to talk with you in the late afternoon, but unless there is an extreme emergency, I need to spend evenings with my family. I avoid taking telephone calls during the time that is reserved for them."

I have found that people are not upset about the time you *cannot* be with them as long as they know when you *can* be with them. When people know what they can count on, it becomes easier for them to wait.

There may be times when you will need to be more available than usual. Be aware, however, that some people will invent a crisis just to get your attention. Do not allow yourself to be directed by the emotional intensity of the person you are helping. You must be led by the Holy Spirit, not the needs of others.

If you receive frequent "crisis" calls for non-emergency situations, you can set a boundary by saying, "This is the time of day when I'm not free to talk. Can you quickly explain the problem to me? What have you already thought about doing?" If your friend gives you a reasonable solution, you might say, "I believe you have already worked this out for yourself. You didn't really need me after all. You had a good idea. I'll be praying for you."

It is your responsibility to teach people to stop, pray and think before automatically calling you. There will be times when you simply cannot be available, and they need to see that they can get along without you.

Once I was working with a woman who left several messages for me each week. I allowed her to do that because I knew that she was in extreme crisis. When the crisis was over, she became offended when I told her to write down all of her questions and bring them to our next session. I had "taught her" that I would be available whenever she decided that she needed me. No human being can offer that kind of availability, so set limits early. If you do not, the person you are helping may assume that you are always on call.

What are the times when you can be most available? What are the times that you absolutely cannot be available? Do you believe that the times you have set are reasonable? Can you stay within those times?

29

"How can I keep the person from becoming too dependent on me?"

Many people who are hurting would like someone to take over and take care of them. Can you remember a time when you wished someone would just come along and make everything all right? Perhaps your parents filled that role when you were a child.

When someone has been enduring a trial for a long time, she may feel as helpless and inadequate as a child. For some of us who want to help, the temptation is to do exactly what she seems to want us to do: take over and take care of the problem. If we do that, however, we will rob the individual of the opportunity to see *God* take over and take care of her. When we try to fill that role, we become *codependent*.

Are there people in your life who create a crisis so that they can have your attention? What do they do? Would you like their behavior to stop? Are you willing to change your own patterns first?

Many sincere helpers fall into codependent relationships because they were family caretakers when they were growing up. Perhaps one of their parents was a substance abuser. Perhaps both parents were physically sick or emotionally unstable. When a child has to take care of adults, she generally continues to assume responsibility for others after she has grown up. Caretakers in this position become excessively burdened by those who rely upon them, but they relish feeling needed and significant. The needy person becomes more and more dependent. In this codependent relationship neither person will grow in Christ. Both people will simply be trusting another human being to meet their needs.

Codependency is a poor imitation of a true spiritual relationship with Jesus, and we do not help anyone when we allow that to happen.

When I was growing up, my mother suffered from depression. Although her condition was never discussed, I was always aware that her emotional state was fragile. I learned how to sense her moods, how to calm her, encourage her, predict and protect her feelings. When she became upset, I took the blame for her behavior, assuring her that whatever happened was all my fault.

When I grew up, I gravitated toward social work, a natural choice for a young caretaker. Within a few years, I realized that there was something amiss. I was burning out and did not know why. I sought God's help and He showed me that I was a well-trained co-dependent. I asked Him to break my cycle of overworking and over-caring.

Have you ever become too dependent upon someone? If so, what was the result of your over-dependence? Have you ever let someone become too dependent upon you? What was the result? For you? For him or her?

One day as I sat in my office, the Holy Spirit led me to read Isaiah 53:4–5. I felt that He wanted me to personalize that Scripture, so as I read it aloud, this is what I read: *Surely Lynda has borne her mother's griefs—sickness, weakness and distress—and carried her mother's sorrows and pain [of punishment]. . . . Lynda was wounded for her mother's transgressions, she was bruised for her mother's guilt and iniquities; the chastisement needful to obtain peace and well-being for her mother was upon Lynda.*

God's words pierced my soul that day. I quickly asked God's forgiveness for assuming that I could carry burdens that only He can carry. I was relieved to know that He was not asking me to do all that I thought He was requiring of me. I immediately resigned from the role of codependent, but it took a while for me to break old habits.

Still, I began to recognize when I was taking too much responsibility for another person and learned how to avoid excessive burdens. As I studied the way Jesus helped people, I found that He took our sins, sicknesses, weaknesses, distresses and guilt on Himself *for only one day*. That was the day of the cross. What would His life have been like if He had continually taken everyone's pain onto Himself every single day as He lived on the earth? If Jesus could not live that way, why do we ever think that we can?

Did you grow up as a caretaker? Have you been described as the "pillar" or "cornerstone" of your family? If so, how does this make you feel? Do you feel as if you are carrying people on your back instead of in your heart? Do you often feel overloaded emotionally?

If you grew up as a caretaker, ask God to show you if you are prone to take too much responsibility for the feelings or actions of others. If you find that you are, I suggest that you read the book *Please Don't Say You Need Me* by Jan Silvious. This is an excellent book for those faced with issues of codependency.

It is important to know what God promises to do, what He is asking us to do and what He is asking others to do. *If we get our responsibilities mixed up, a helping relationship will go downhill quickly because another person's life is far too heavy for us to carry.*

"How can I be honest without offending?"

If you are going to help someone, there will undoubtedly be times when you must confront behavior. For example, Sally had been helping her sister, Cheryl, learn to stop overspending. After they had reviewed Cheryl's income and debts, they made a budget. For a while, Cheryl kept her spending under control, but when her boyfriend broke up with her, she returned automatically to her old method of self-comfort: shopping. After one long excursion to the mall, she called Sally and excitedly described her purchases.

Sally was quiet for a moment, praying. She did not want to hurt Cheryl, but she knew that Cheryl's euphoria was going to be temporary. Soon the bills would have to be paid.

First, Sally reminded Cheryl of the progress she had made. Then she took a deep breath and said, "You have made so many good decisions about money during the last few weeks. Isn't this the first time you've gone on a spending spree?"

Cheryl was silent. Suddenly she realized what she had done! In her effort to comfort herself, she had fallen back into

Have you observed this type of growth pattern in yourself? Others? If so, can you identify some specific patterns in yourself or others?

an old bondage and ended up at a familiar, destructive place. Cheryl realized that she wanted to get back on track. With Sally's encouragement she returned most of her purchases, and they prayed together that night, releasing Cheryl's hurt feelings to Jesus and praying for His comfort to sustain her.

When we have seen steps toward progress, we tend to be surprised when someone slips back into an old pattern. Most of us, however, take a few steps forward and then fall back a few steps. That is the way people grow.

When someone falls back into old behaviors, I suggest that you address the issue from a positive point as Sally did, reminding your friend of the good choices she has recently made. Most likely, your friend will recognize what she has done and want to correct her behavior. If she does not, you might ask, "How do you think you'll feel tomorrow? Will this really comfort you? It's not too late to turn things around, if you want to do so." You will be offering her a tactful invitation to think about her actions and their consequences.

Do you feel anxious when you hear the word confrontation? *If so, what comes to mind?*

What should you do if she dodges the issue? You will need to be honest in a kind way. You could say, "If we are going to work together, I need to be honest with you. I don't want to see you hurt anymore. Would you like to hear what I think?"

If your friend is open to corrective action, your confrontation will have helped her meet her goals. If she is not open, you will simply need to release her to do whatever she wants to do. (We will discuss letting go in chapter 3, "Creating a Climate for Change.")

"What if I have to break a promise?"

Be careful about making promises. People who are hurting tend to hang onto every word you say. They look forward to your doing what you say you are going to do. James 4:13–15 tells us,

Come now, you who say, Today or tomorrow we will go into such and such a city and spend a year there and carry on our business and make money. Yet you do not know [the least thing] about what may happen tomorrow. What is the nature of your life? . . . You ought instead to say, If the Lord is willing, we shall live and we shall do this or that [thing].

You may save yourself some difficulty if you follow James' instructions.

You can, however, make conditional promises such as "If I don't have to work late tomorrow night, I would like to meet you for dinner. Would it be all right if I call you tomorrow afternoon and let you know for sure?" If you cannot meet for dinner, you have already prepared your friend. You have also given him a chance to make other plans if he chooses to do so.

Has someone ever said to you, "But you promised me?" How did you feel? How did the person appear to feel?

People who have been hurt do not trust easily. That is another reason why you need to be careful. If you break your promises, you can hamper someone's ability to learn to trust again.

"What should I do about lending money?"

Money can be a tricky issue. Many people going through a crisis are having financial problems that may not have been preventable.

Suppose, for example, that someone is sick and misses work. He may not only lose income for the days not worked but also may find that his insurance is not going to cover the medical expenses. Or he might need additional income to hire someone to help with tasks at home.

If you believe that God is asking you to help someone financially, I suggest that you simply *give him or her the money.* Then the issue is settled. If you loan money and he cannot pay you back, he will feel embarrassed. You may begin to wonder if he is making the effort to pay you back. Addressing issues about money can be awkward and can burden a relationship.

If, on the other hand, someone has been spending unwisely, it would be foolish to give him more money. You would only be enabling him to continue the same harmful behavior that caused the problem. Although it can be painful to watch someone suffer the consequences of his actions, remember that pain can be a good teacher. By not giving him money, you can make a good contribution toward his growth and maturity in financial matters.

Have you ever regretted lending money to someone? If so, why?

"How will I know if the person needs professional help? If so, what then?"

There will be times when those who are suffering need professional help. If you are aware that someone is spiraling downward into depression, you have reason for concern. Listen carefully for despondent remarks such as "Everyone would be better off without me" or "Life is just too hard. I don't have anything to live for now." Comments like these can indicate suicidal thoughts. At that point, you should tell her that she needs more help than you know how to give.

Suggest that your friend visit a professional counselor. If she is unwilling to take that step alone, ask if she would be willing for you to find a good counselor. Offer to go with her for her first visit.

Until your friend has her first appointment, arrange to have someone with her at vulnerable times. If you truly believe that your friend may endanger herself, inform her family. (Even professionals are released from confidentiality if a life is in danger.) Your friend may become angry, but her survival is more important than her temporary feelings of anger toward you.

> *Do you feel as if you would be insulting or belittling someone if you suggest that she needs professional help? If so, why? Are your feelings legitimate or not? Is it shameful to need professional help?*

"What if the person resists getting professional help?"

People who are suicidal are often impulsive. If you have informed her family, you might also find it helpful to get a suicidal person to make an agreement with you that may create a pause between a suicidal thought and a destructive action. For example, you might ask, "Will you promise to call me if you become tempted to hurt yourself?" Set up specific times that you will see her every day. Knowing that she will see you soon may also enable her to delay a destructive impulse.

> *Have you ever known someone who was suicidal? How did you know that he was? When you realized his life was in danger, how did you feel?*

"When do I override his hesitation to get professional help?"

A young pastor named Sam had been meeting regularly with a young man, Peter, who was depressed. Sam thought that Peter had made significant progress, but when Peter returned from a visit to his parents' home, his mood began to sink again. Nothing Sam did or said seemed to have an impact on him.

One morning when Sam met Peter for breakfast, he noticed that Peter appeared to be greatly improved, almost euphoric.

Some people would assume that Peter's sudden change of mood was a good sign, but a sudden, strong shift from depression into euphoria can be a signal that someone has decided how and when to die. The mood change is not true improvement. Instead, it is an expression of relief that comes from knowing their pain will soon be over.

Because Sam recognized the signs of a possible impending suicide attempt, he questioned Peter. He found that Peter had cleaned out his apartment, written some letters and set aside a couple of special mementos for friends. At that point, Sam insisted that Peter accompany him to the nearest emergency room. Peter agreed to go.

Why would someone who has decided to kill himself give up a plan to die so easily? *People who are contemplating suicide do not really want to die; they want to get out of pain.* That is why Peter gave in when Sam insisted upon getting immediate relief.

On the way to the hospital, Sam told Peter about the various new medications for depression. He informed him that, with proper medical care, Peter could begin to come out of his emotional darkness within a few weeks. Then he could begin to work on his problems on a deeper, professional level.

More than anything, Peter needed relief and Sam offered him a concrete, immediate way to receive it. If you are helping someone like Peter, do not hesitate to act.

First Corinthians 10:13 says,

For no temptation—no trial regarded as enticing to sin [no matter how it comes or where it leads]—has overtaken you and laid hold on you that is not common to man—that is, no temptation or trial has come to you that is beyond human resistance. . . . But God is faithful . . . He will [always] also provide the way out—the means of escape to a landing place—that you may be capable and strong and powerful patiently to bear up under it.

If someone you are helping is not improving, pray for God to show you the way out that He has provided. In a kind but firm manner, compel your friend to go to a safe landing place. People who are depressed are also confused. They are unable to seek solutions and make good decisions. At times like this, you need to set the direction and take action.

If a suicidal person refuses help, it is wise to consult a mental health professional. An intervention might be planned, which could include family members, a pastor, a family physician, friends and the mental health professional. Sometimes the influence of a group can have a powerfully persuasive impact.

However, nobody can guard a suicidal person every moment of the day and night. In Deuteronomy 30:19 God says, "I have set before you life and death . . . therefore choose life, that you and your descendants may live." Each person is given the choice by God to live or die. When all efforts have been made, the helpers must grant a loved one the same choice.

Also, if your friend is suicidal be prepared to answer the question, "Do people who kill themselves go to heaven?"

The sixth Commandment, "You shall not murder," means that we should not kill anyone, not even ourselves. Suicide is definitely not God's will. One of Satan's cruelest lies is that we can cease to exist. He convinces us that if we can destroy our bodies, we can destroy ourselves. This is not true. We will not cease to exist. We will, however, change locations and there is no guarantee that we will not still be in pain. If a suicidal person can grasp this truth, he will likely agree to receive help.

Have you ever been asked if people who kill themselves go to heaven? If so, how did you respond? What do you believe? Which Scriptures have given you that belief?

Inform your friend that, according to Scripture, we are all going to live somewhere forever. We are not going to cease to exist. *We are going to be who we are forever . . . somewhere.*

I hope that these questions and answers have helped alleviate some of your concerns about helping others. Knowing how to respond to a call for help can not only encourage you to move ahead with confidence and assurance but can make you more effective. Let us continue now with one of the most vital tools of helping: learning how to be a good listener.

TWO

Listening—A Cornerstone of Helping

Each week I take part in a "growth group" of about a dozen women who are seeking ways to become the best they can be in specific areas of their lives. Many are in periods of transition.

During a recent time together, God taught us a lesson on listening. One of the women, Teresa, had just been abandoned by her husband. He had left her and their three teenagers for his high school sweetheart.

Teresa wiped away tears as she told her story: "I don't think I can raise three children by myself. I can't believe he left us! I married him when we were both barely out of high school, so we've been together for all of our adult lives. He's always been there. I don't know how I can live without him!"

While Teresa was speaking, another group member named Angela had begun turning through the pages of her Bible. Just as Teresa paused, Angela sprang forward, Bible in hand. She exclaimed, "Teresa, everything will be all right! The Bible says that Jesus will be your husband, and He is the father of the fatherless!"

As Angela began to read from her Bible, Teresa held up her hand to silence her. "Of course I know what the Bible says! Right now, I don't *care!* I want my flesh-and-blood husband back in our home! Can't you see? *My heart is broken!* I'm trying to tell you how I feel and you aren't listening. I don't want to hear anything else you have to say." She turned her back toward Angela.

Have you ever found yourself formulating answers at the same time you were listening to someone? Have you ever moved to the edge of your seat so that you could break into the conversation as quickly as possible? Has anyone ever cut you off in order to tell you what she thinks you need to know? How did you feel?

Angela froze, dumbfounded. She clearly did not understand what had happened. Had she not used God's Word to help Teresa? Her intention was to comfort and reassure, but her words had created even more distress and anguish. *What had she done wrong?*

As we will see, she had not followed the rules of good listening. Her efforts, though meant to be caring, actually expressed inconsiderate behavior.

A Lesson Learned

An old saying goes, "People don't care what you know until they know that you care." Making the effort to listen is one of the richest gifts we can give someone who is troubled. Listening proves that we care. It is the first step to helping.

Several years ago, one of my clients showed me a valuable lesson. On the day that she came for her counseling session, I had just returned from a conference and was exhausted. She talked and talked and talked. Before I realized it, the hour was up and the session was over. After she left, I thought, *I sure didn't give her much this time.* I regretted that I had not offered her pertinent information or formulated an assignment for her.

When this client returned the next week, she greeted me with enthusiasm. She exclaimed, "Last week was the best session we've ever had! I felt so loved when I left your office!"

She continued, "As I talked to you last week, I was able to see how negative my thinking had become. My bitterness was obvious! As I listened to myself, there was no way I could deny it. This week, I let God deal with me about that."

And then she made the most important observation of all: "I realized that the answers were really already inside of me. I just needed to unload the layers that were pushing them down. After I unloaded, I could begin to hear His voice."

This client helped me understand that most of us already have the answers we need deep down inside. Often we just need someone to listen, to allow us to unload our emotions so that we, too, can hear ourselves.

Proverbs 8:34 says, "Blessed . . . is the man who listens." Listening is hard work. It takes our total focus. It is also an act of self-denial because if we listen well, we must put our own thoughts, opinions and reactions aside.

Why are so many of us poor listeners? I believe, for starters, that we are not convinced that listening really helps people. Rather than let the person explore his own thoughts by our silence or considerate comments, we begin pouring out information.

Do you believe that listening is truly valuable? Has talking to someone ever helped you? If so, how? Do you believe that giving information is more important than listening?

We are also poor listeners because we do not discipline ourselves to do it. I am a high-energy person, and it is difficult for me simply to sit and listen for long periods of time. New ideas jump in my mind like popcorn in a popper. It is a huge challenge either to remain silent or to respond with words that help the individual continue to think things through. In fact, it probably takes more discipline for me to be still than it takes to lecture for two hours in a seminar! Listening is truly a sacrifice for me, but I know that I must do it. In order to help people feel loved, I must allow them to feel, to unload and to offer their own conclusions.

Listening is not the time to give suggestions, share your own experiences or offer encouragement. Listening is simply that . . . *listening*. If it is difficult for you to listen, remember that God will reward you for your discipline.

How Can I Help Someone Unload?

Listening is a skill; therefore, it is something that each one of us can learn to do. Here are some principles to guide you as you help individuals unload the burdens they carry.

Clarify what you think the person said.

After Angela's misguided efforts to help Teresa, Angela, as well as other group members, realized that a different approach to listening was needed. One woman got things on the right track when she said, "Teresa, let me make sure I know everything you need me to know. Your husband has been with you since high school and now he has left you, and you don't know what you will do without him. You have children to raise and the future seems impossible. He has broken your heart." As she repeated what she remembered from Teresa's words, Teresa began visibly to relax. She took a deep breath, sat back in her chair and replied, "Yes, that's what I said." She seemed no longer to feel isolated and misunderstood.

When you are listening, do you fidget? Look around the room? Are you easily distracted? Will you discipline yourself to be still?

Then another member stated, "If I were in your place right now, I would be afraid, too." She did not present solutions or remind Teresa about God's promises to be present during times of fear. She simply listened and identified. *She stayed with Teresa just where she was.* I know that this woman had many helpful things she could have said, but she was wise enough to refrain from saying them until Teresa indicated she was ready to receive help.

Do not make assumptions.

Have you ever told someone, "I know just how you feel"? I have, and it was a bad mistake. The woman to whom I was speaking informed me that there was no way I could know

45

exactly how she felt, even though my past circumstances mirrored hers. I realized that what she said was true. We are all different, and we will not perceive circumstances in the same way, no matter how similar they may be. Our emotional responses will be different due to our personalities and our histories, as well as our levels of spiritual maturity.

Jesus is the only one who knows how we really feel. Hebrews 4:15 says, "For we do not have a High Priest Who is unable to understand and sympathize and have a fellow feeling with our weaknesses and infirmities and liability to the assaults of temptation, but One Who has been tempted in every respect as we are, yet without sinning."

Have you ever said, "I know exactly how you feel"? Was that a true statement? How do you think the other person felt when you said that?

Because Jesus is well acquainted with what we experience in life on earth, He is merciful and invites us to "confidently and boldly draw near to the throne of grace" (verse 16). He promises that we will find His mercy for our failures and His well-timed help, coming just when we need it!

We can say that we have some degree of understanding and identification with those in need, but only Jesus, who lives in our hearts by the power of the Holy Spirit, truly experiences our feelings along with us.

It is not wise to speak carelessly. As James 1:19 advises us, "Let every man be quick to hear, (a ready listener,) slow to speak."

Pray for a good sense of timing.

The right thing said prematurely is not helpful. Later in our group discussion that morning, Teresa said, "I need to find peace. I really need some help."

That was the signal the group had been waiting for . . . a sign that Teresa had unloaded enough emotion to receive help from us. We began to offer a few suggestions.

When we try to move people along too quickly, they stall and become stuck where they are, feeling that they have not been heard. Until they are ready to move ahead, they may dig in their heels and become more and more frustrated.

Ask good questions.

When our group had clarified Teresa's story, someone asked, "What do you need the most right now?" Teresa spoke with more assurance as her energy and concentration focused on giving factual information about her circumstances. She said, "I feel so sad and afraid, but I know I have to find a job. I haven't worked in years." Her emotional intensity decreased. She was able to begin defining a specific need.

Do not censor.

Recently a man named Joe whose wife had left him told me about his experience with poor listeners: "I was angry and upset. I knew that my wife left because I had not been a good husband. Actually, I've been a jerk much of our married life! I was mad at myself for failing and I was mad at her for leaving.

"I had promised to go to my men's group that morning. I was embarrassed to go, but I had made a commitment to attend every week so I went. When my friends asked me how things were going, I expressed my anger. Immediately one of the men folded his hands together, leaned forward and said, 'Now Joe, it won't do you any good to talk about her. You need to take a good look at yourself.'"

47

Joe continued, "At that point, I wished I had not come. I knew what my friend was saying was true, but I really needed to let off some steam! I wanted to yell, 'Won't you please just listen?' Not only was I angry with myself and my wife, but I was angry with them, too. I didn't say another word."

Avoid pat answers.

A worried mom named Sandra told me the following: "I was afraid that my teenage daughter was on drugs. When I told my prayer group what I feared, one member said to me, 'A few years ago, I thought my daughter might be on drugs. I just prayed about it and didn't worry. Just pray about it. God will take care of your daughter.'"

Sandra said, "If there's one thing that turns me off, it's pat answers!" Platitudes are often shallow and rarely on target because they take into account only a portion of the truth. In this case the truth was that God would influence Sandra's daughter, but her daughter also had the God-given right to exercise her free will, which might invite a period of drug use. Pat answers belittle and silence people.

Has someone ever censored your words? If so, how did you feel? Have you censored someone? If so, what effect did it have?

Watch for unspoken words.

Once a middle-aged man named Jeff said, "It doesn't matter that I lost that job! I was sick of it anyway. I'm glad to be out of there. Now I can find a job I really like."

I would have believed Jeff if he had not spoken through clenched teeth. When he banged his right fist into the palm of his left hand several times, I *knew* that he was not letting himself speak truthfully.

Sometimes our bodies speak more clearly than our words. I have observed clients who wring their hands with worry, saying that they are trusting God. Others cross their arms tightly across their chests as if they are afraid to let themselves talk or even feel.

Have you ever given anyone a pat answer and then realized that your words had offended? How did you know? Has anyone ever done that to you? Can you recognize how your own body language might deny your words?

When you are with someone who may not be revealing his true feelings, ask God for wisdom. You need to know if it is time to ask for more information, to present a challenge or to confront. It is usually best to let someone set his own pace, but there are times when we need to press past appearances.

Keep confidentiality.

For anyone to speak freely to you, he or she must feel safe. Often the deepest needs are not expressed because of lack of trust.

Recently after I spoke at a conference, a woman confided, "I committed a sin over a year ago that continues to bother me. I have not been able to get over the guilt and shame, even though I know what Scripture teaches about God's forgiveness, cleansing and mercy. I am afraid to talk to anyone at my church because, somehow or other, information always leaks out. A friend told me that if I had private things to discuss I should go to a professional counselor. Are the only people who can be trusted those who are legally bound to keep silent?"

Keeping confidentiality calls for denial of self. We must discipline the impulse to reveal secret knowledge. Some believers tend to act impulsively in various areas of their lives and breaking confidentiality may be one of those areas. If you know that you tend to act impulsively, be very careful when you agree to keep a matter confidential.

Why do you think believers often handle private information so carelessly? Do we need to be bound by law in order to be trusted?

You may need to disqualify yourself from listening to highly confidential information until you mature more in that area. Find other ways to be of service; do not endanger someone who needs help.

By the same token, do not listen to information that others are supposed to be keeping confidential. A woman named Janice said, "A friend of mine started to tell me something that she had been told in confidence. She began by saying, 'I'm not supposed to tell you this, but I just can't carry this burden alone. I need you to pray with me about this.'"

We cannot spiritualize breaking confidentiality. If we have said that we will not reveal information, we must not reveal it. Often we are simply yielding to the desire to gossip.

God Is the Best Listener

Some of us find it easier to talk to a flesh-and-blood person than to a God we cannot see. However, He is the only one who will always be available to listen. His sense

50

of timing is perfect. He knows our histories, our present and future. He knows each person who has been involved in our lives. He has all the facts. He knows what must be done. His motives and judgments are always accurate.

The most valuable lesson you can teach the person you are helping is to teach her to pray. Tell her that she has an ongoing invitation to enter the throne room of God (see Hebrews 4:16). She may stay as long as she wants. She may talk as long as she wants. God never turns His ear away from His children. God will hear.

Then teach her to listen to God, for He will respond. Matthew 11:15 admonishes us, "He who has ears to hear, let him be listening, and consider and perceive and comprehend by hearing." As she enters the throne room and remains still, the Holy Spirit will speak to her spirit.

THREE

CREATING A CLIMATE FOR CHANGE

Several years ago, due to a severe spine injury, I was sent to see a highly recommended physical therapist named Jason. During my initial session Jason asked, "What do you hope to accomplish while we work together?"

I responded quickly, "I want to become pain-free for life!"

Jason leaned back in his chair, looked me in the eye and replied, "Well, that may be possible, but if it is going to happen, you're going to need a strong desire because you have a lot of work ahead of you! I will help you, but most of the work will be yours."

Then he paused and asked, "On a scale of one-to-ten, with ten being the highest desire, how would you rank your desire for recovery?"

Again, I responded quickly, "My desire is a ten-plus." Jason smiled as if to say, Well, we'll see if it stays that way!

Jason was honest with me. He did not give me pat answers or empty encouragement. My task was clearly defined. He put the responsibility on me. He did not present himself as the noble hero who would carry me through, and I understood that, with God's help, it was up to me.

As I began the therapy, I realized that his words had been absolutely true. The path was going to be long and difficult. If progress was going to be made, my resolve would have to remain strong.

Likewise, in a helping relationship, it is important for you to make this point clear. *You are simply the helper; the other person has primary responsibility for the process of change.*

Good Questions to Ask

When you are working with someone who is in difficult circumstances, it is often wise to do exactly what Jason did: Give the person you are helping an opportunity to test his or her own level of desire. Whether one wants to strengthen a spine, break a habit or overcome a tragedy, the desire must be strong.

Here are some questions that will serve as good "responsibility checks" for the person you are helping.

What do you really want?

Many people know that they want relief from pain, but past that point, few actually know what they really want.

For example, Rose had been married for years to Eric, who had been involved in many extramarital affairs. She had recently graduated from a nearby university when she found out that he had been involved with one of the female students there.

Rose was hurt and disillusioned. Once again, trust in her husband had been destroyed. She asked me, "How can I save this marriage?" Yet when I asked Rose to consider what she wanted, she thought a moment and replied, "Well, I have a degree now and I can probably get a good job. Honestly, I would rather end this marriage than put my trust in a lying man again."

Because Rose wanted to leave Eric *more* than she wanted to put trust in him again, it would have been useless to try to help her build the trust that might save her marriage. Many people are like Rose. They may think or say they want one thing, but, deep down, they really want something else.

In order to help, you must know what a person wants for her life and then you must decide if you can support that desire. You may be tempted to reason or coerce someone into a better decision, but in the long run, that decision will not stick. The person will hold you responsible for the time she has lost, as well as any unnecessary pain she suffered if she yields to pressure from you.

Have you ever tried to convince someone to do something he did not really want to do? If so, what happened? Have you ever felt pressured by someone else? Was that person helpful to you? Why do we try to "make" people do what we think they should do?

How much do you want it?

I suggest that you use the "one-to-ten scale" to define the level of desire the person has about change. Remember that change requires strong motivation. Once your friend knows what she wants, how much does she really want it?

Are you willing to do whatever it may take?

For most of us, there is usually a point of resistance beyond which we do not want to go. When asked this question, many people can identify that point quickly.

For example, I asked Rick if there was anything he would not be willing to do. He said, "Yes, there is just one thing. Don't ever ask me to speak to my father again."

I responded, "God may not require that you speak to your father again, but if doing so will help you become whole, He probably will prompt you to do so. *Regardless, those who are willing to do whatever it takes are the ones who get better the fastest.*" Resistance limits progress.

If the person you are helping can identify steps he is not willing to take, ask if he is willing to ask God to change his mind. Use Proverbs 16:3 as a prayer: "Roll your works upon the Lord—commit and trust them wholly to Him; [He will cause your thoughts to become agreeable to His will, and] so shall your plans be established and succeed." God can change desires that are submitted to Him.

In addition, Philippians 2:13 makes it clear that God can *increase* desire: "[Not in your own strength] for it is God Who is all the while effectually at work in you—energizing and creating in you the power and desire—both to will and to work for His good pleasure and satisfaction and delight."

Remember that even our desires can come from God. If there is not enough longing in our hearts, we can ask for more, if we are willing to submit to Him.

What do you need from me?

It is helpful to you, as well as to the one you are helping, to know what your responsibilities will be. Expectations should be clearly defined.

For example, Emily told Fran that it would be helpful if she would pray for her each day, and call her
weekly. She also asked for permission to call Fran in
times of crisis. That was agreeable with Fran, so Emily
and Fran both knew what to expect.

Are you ready to begin the process of changing?

If there is a strong desire, and God leads, make a
commitment to accompany the person toward the
changes he or she wants to make.

The Process of Changing

Now you are ready to begin helping your friend enter
the process of changing toward wholeness. There seems
to be an ebb and flow to helping. These directions will
help you maximize your time and efforts so that
progress can be made more easily.

Set some short-term goals.

Because it is encouraging to experience some success,
set goals that can be achieved easily. Keep your agree-
ments simple. People do not make flying leaps toward
change. You might plan to meet once a week or agree
to pray about a particular issue.

I have a dear friend, Carole, who is a counselor. She
tells the story of a man who sold computer software.
Much of his inventory was outdated, but he was unwill-

ing to invest in more inventory until he sold more of his current stock. Carole could see that he was stuck. It was time for him to move forward. Seeing that his inventory was a stumbling block, she suggested that he simply throw his old inventory away! The man turned pale, absolutely refused and remained stuck for several more weeks. Finally, he was able to throw it away in stages. He could take small steps but could not make a giant leap.

It is helpful to ask "What is a small step you can take now?" or "What could be the next step?"

Recognize and build on strengths.

Most of us fail initially because of our sinful nature, weaknesses, ignorance, lack of knowledge and self-will. Even though there will be successes, the path toward change will include some failure. In the beginning, desire, dependency on God, effort and consistency are what count. In fact, for a while there may be more failure than success.

When we recognize that failure is part of the journey, we are not disillusioned when we fall. Most of us do not realize how weak we really are until we try to change a behavior. Identifying strengths is a good way to overcome discouragement.

A pastor was meeting weekly with a young man who had just lost his third job in a year. The pastor reached across the table, took the young man's hand and said, "Son, you may have lost another job, but I've never seen anybody who is better at getting jobs than you are. You have a friendly manner that people really like. Use that trait to get your next job. You have a few things to learn. We'll learn them together and you should be able to do well."

The young man was encouraged and able to gather the strength to go try again.

Avoid comparisons.

Remember that no two people are alike. We can never know the entire history of another human being. What appears to be poor progress may actually be excellent progress, considering where someone began.

For instance, one person who needs your support to stop smoking may be able to stop within a month. Another person who wants to stop smoking may not have the confidence, discipline or motivation required for success. Her journey may be longer and harder.

If you compare the progress of one person to that of another, you will most likely draw incorrect conclusions and become impatient and discouraged.

Initiate prayer times of confession and petition.

When failure has occurred, help the person discern whether or not he bears some responsibility in what happened. If he did, encourage him to take responsibility for that. If restitution is needed, encourage him to make things right. If he is willing, take the issue before God and pray together. Encourage him to ask God for instructions and make a plan to do things differently next time.

Allow people to have "soaking" time.

No matter how strong our desire to grow may be, we all need plateaus. We cannot process new truth and practice new behavior without taking a few rest stops along the way to soak in the change.

Tom had met with Hank once a week for two months. He commented, "For the first few weeks, Hank was really moving on! He was eager to learn. Now it seems as if he is just maintaining. I'm getting concerned."

Tom did not realize that maintenance is progress! If we can master a change and maintain the change, that is reason for celebration.

Compassion versus Judgment

One of the most common stumbling blocks to helping others is judgment. Unfortunately, judgment thrives in the Church.

Recently I was eating alone in a restaurant and overheard the conversation of a group of women in the booth behind me. It was obvious that they had just learned that one of their friends had had an affair.

One woman exclaimed, "I just don't see how she could have done that. You'd think she'd have better sense! I hope she is wallowing in guilt."

Another added, "Well, I thought she had more sense than that, too! Honestly, I don't want to have anything else to do with her anymore."

And on they went, pouring judgment and rejection on the friend.

Is it possible to reject a sinner and help a sinner at the same time? Have you ever refused to associate with someone because of her sin? Were you willing to find out if she wanted help?

Often we judge others and do not even realize it. Statements that express judgment sound like this:

"How could you have done that?"
"I can't believe you did that!"

"That was so stupid!"

"You got exactly what you deserved!"

"You'll have to pay!"

"You don't deserve another chance!"

"I should have known you were that way!"

"You'll never change."

Romans 14:11–13 states:

> For it is written, As I live, says the Lord, every knee shall bow to Me, and every tongue shall confess to God—that is, acknowledge Him to His honor and to His praise. And so each of us shall give an account of himself—give an answer in reference to judgment—to God. Then let us no more criticize and blame and pass judgment on one another, but rather decide and endeavor never to put a stumbling block or an obstacle or a hindrance in the way of a brother.

Have you found yourself expressing judgment? Has anyone judged you? If so, how did you feel? Was the judgment encouraging to you? Did it motivate you to change?

Our job is to leave the way open for repentance and watch for opportunities to help someone who has fallen. Judgment is God's job, not ours. It can be a stumbling block.

Why do we judge?

Sometimes we judge people because we do not see ourselves clearly and we have a superior opinion of ourselves.

Jesus' words from Matthew 7:3–5 explain the folly of our pride:

Why do you stare from without at the very small particle that is in your brother's eye, but do not become aware of and consider the beam of timber that is in your own eye? Or how can you say to your brother, Let me get the tiny particle out of your eye, when there is the beam of timber in your own eye? You hypocrite, first get the beam of timber out of your own eye, and then you will see clearly to take the tiny particle out of your brother's eye.

Have you ever observed someone's behavior and murmured, "Well, at least I don't do that!"? Have you ever been surprised later by your own behavior? Can you give an example? Have you found it convenient to judge?

Recently I criticized the offensive behavior of a friend. Later that week, I did the same thing she had done! Immediately my words came back to haunt me. I had been surprised at her behavior, and later I was surprised at mine. I had a hidden beam in my own eye! I had no room to judge her.

If we can find something in another person that is worse than what we can see in ourselves, we can feel more comfortable in our own sinful behavior and attitudes. When we do this, we simply use another person to excuse ourselves.

Remember that judging is dangerous.

In Matthew 7:1–2 Jesus' words warn us:

Do not judge and criticize and condemn others, so that you may not be judged and criticized and condemned yourselves. For just as you judge and criticize and condemn others, you will be judged and criticized and condemned, and in accordance with the measure you deal out to others it will be dealt out again to you.

When I realized that I had exhibited the same behavior that I had judged my friend for exhibiting, I wondered if the one I had offended would give more mercy to me than I had given to my friend.

Offer statements of compassion.

Compassionate words bring great hope to one who has failed. These statements do not express judgment or condemnation:

"I'm so sorry to hear that."
"It makes me sad to know this."
"I'll be with you."
"Regardless, I believe in you."
"We can see this through together."
"I have failed, too. I know it hurts. I will pray for you."
"I'm sorry you are hurting now."

Matthew 9:36 says that Jesus was moved by compassion. In 1 Samuel 16:7, God said to Samuel, "The Lord sees not as man sees; for man looks on the outward appearance, but the Lord looks on the heart."

We will never know anyone's history and heart as God does. That is why we are not qualified nor allowed to judge others. We will never have all the facts about another person's life.

Avoid punishing.

When we judge we are not willing to be patient with people. We want them to shape up . . . now. It becomes difficult for us to wait for God's kindness and mercy to do its work.

We may become angry and sincerely want to make the offender pay. However, we must learn to leave such issues in God's hands. Romans 2:6 assures us that He will execute proper judgment in a compassionate manner: "For He will render to every man according to his works—justly, as his deeds deserve."

Can you recall times in your own life when you have failed? Were you hoping to find mercy from God and those around you? Did you find it? If not, is it possible that you were receiving the fruit of your own lack of mercy?

Sometimes when we think someone should be punished, we find ways to do so, either directly or indirectly. We may openly administer the pain that we think God should inflict upon him by judging him or verbally shaming him. Indirect punishment is sometimes achieved through gossip and criticism. No matter how the punishment is inflicted, judging is sinful and its results are destructive.

Through constant prayer, we can become aware of our judgmental attitudes and offer compassion instead, keeping the relational climate open for change to occur.

Recognize and address sin.

Although we should not judge, we can address sinful behavior. That can be done simply by asking, "Do you believe that you are doing anything wrong?" or "Do you think some of the responsibility may belong to you?"

Look at Scripture together to determine whether or not an action is sinful. If you determine that sin is evident, ask, "Would you like to make this right? Do you want to change?"

If the one you are helping does not wish to repent or change, remember that his life belongs to him, not to you. Release him again to God's care. Pray and let God work.

If They Don't Change, What Then?

There are people who decide they are not willing to do the work that is required. If you believe that the person you are helping has lost his desire, simply ask, "Where are you right now on the one-to-ten scale of your desire to make the change you initially wanted to make?" This is a quick way to help someone decide whether or not he wants to continue.

Then ask, "Do you believe you have made any progress?" If progress has been made, recognize it and give credit to God for His support. Also give credit to the one you are helping.

If there is not a strong desire, you may want to suggest that your meetings or communications be postponed for a while. Do not make a promise to continue at a later date unless you are sure that you can be available.

Remember: Ceasing contact is not rejection. We must be careful that we do not convey rejection.

Be sure to express love and goodwill, but in a helping relationship, when you are no longer allowed to help, your primary purpose has been completed.

For example, Monica had been helping Joyce through bitterness after a divorce. Joyce broke several luncheon meetings. Sensing that Joyce's desire to meet was no longer strong, Monica said, "You made so much progress when you kept our appointments and fulfilled your reading assignments. Could we just take a time-out until you are ready to continue? If I can be available to you then, we can continue together."

Sometimes you need to release the person you are helping to God and leave the outcome there. Remember that your role was to be available to help—not to make someone change. The responsibility for change rests totally on God and the other person.

It is helpful to read and share with your friend the statement that Paul made when he left his friends:

What might happen if you fail to suggest a time-out? How could taking a time-out benefit the one you have been helping? How could it benefit you?

> And now, brethren, I commit you to God—that is, I deposit you in His charge, entrusting you to His protection and care. And I commend you to the Word of His grace—to the commands and counsels and promises of His unmerited favor. It is able to build you up and to give you [your rightful] inheritance among all God's set-apart ones—those consecrated, purified and transformed of soul.
>
> Acts 20:32

As you leave your friend in God's care, express your love and give your blessing over his or her life.

You may never know the full effect you have had on someone's life. In a time of need, you planted seeds of love that can result in change even years later. Prayers that you have said can still be answered in the future. The love you have given will never lose its power.

Your responsibility is to love. God will perform the changes as your hurting friend allows Him to work. Remember that God loves even more than you do, and that He will complete the good work that He began (see Philippians 1:6).

FOUR

HOW TO PERSEVERE

If we are going to maintain our willingness to help others, we must decide to be as considerate of ourselves as we are the ones we are helping. If not, we will develop the condition known as "burnout."

Not long ago, I was nearing the end of a busy season of work. I was tired. I knew I had been on overload for quite some time. I had booked too many clients and had not given myself enough time to recuperate following weekend seminars. When I checked my answering machine, I would sigh inwardly at the number of calls I needed to return. My batteries were running low, and it was getting harder and harder for me to persevere. I was receiving warnings, and I knew that I was not being a good friend to myself.

During those long days, I had a counseling appointment with a woman who had been having an affair for several months. She was middle-aged, pretty and vivacious. Even though she felt guilty about the affair, she was still in the stage of infatuation and deception. She could not make up her mind about whether or not to end it. I was beginning to feel that coming to me was simply the price she made herself pay for continuing the affair. I also believed that seeing me helped her convince herself that she was "doing something" about her situation.

As she began to talk that day, I grew impatient with her. I was also feeling impatient with myself because I had not been able to help her decide to end the affair. I had begun to carry a burden that God had not asked me to carry—the burden of her behavior. We were both stuck, and because I was on the edge of burnout, I was of no help to her or myself.

I remember another telling example. Years ago when I worked in the area of child abuse, my partner and I were discussing the behavior of an abusive mother. My partner said, "When I hear her continue to yell at those kids, I feel like yelling at her! I'm afraid I'll become as abusive to her as she is to her children!" She was burning out, and it was becoming evident.

Have you or anyone you know ever experienced burnout? If so, what were the symptoms? What type of circumstances preceded the burnout?

If you find, as we did in these cases, that anger and impatience are growing toward the individual you are committed to helping, you must turn from the path of certain burnout. This is for everyone's protection. If your inner resources are depleted, you are liable to do more harm than good.

Various clues can tell us we are wearing out. We need to learn to recognize them before we lose the edge of endurance. First we will look at these clues. Next we will address what to do about burnout. Lastly, we will learn how to help others persevere.

Clues That Indicate Burnout

Take a few moments to ponder these emotions and see if you recognize them in yourself, like I did, in a current helping situation.

Impatience—In the example on the previous page, my feelings of impatience toward my client were evident. I was tired of listening to her ambivalence.

Anger—If I had not caught myself in time, my impatience with my client would have turned into anger. I would probably have thought, *Why can't she make up her mind? Why does she even come here if she doesn't want help?*

Self-pity—In my extreme fatigue I felt sorry for myself. I thought, *I've done all this work with this woman, and I've just wasted my time.*

Ingratitude—If we are truly serving, then getting gratitude and appreciation is not our motive. However, I was tired and I did not feel appreciated. I wanted the person I was helping to realize how much work I had done. I even thought that if she realized how hard I had tried to help her, she would make a final decision to end the affair. That kind of pressure never truly inspires anyone.

Self-condemnation—If we do not blame the person we are helping, we are prone to blame ourselves. I might have thought, *If I were a better counselor, she wouldn't be stuck and I wouldn't either. Why am I in this business, anyway? I can't help anybody.*

A "Prescription" for Burnout

Do these negative attitudes ring any bells? If they do—now or in the future—you need to follow the only prescription that works for burnout: Take a break! Think about what is restful for you and do it. One man expressed it this way: "It's time for me to go fishing!" For one helper, it might be time to get a massage. For another helper, it might be time to curl up with a good mystery book.

When we deeply care about others, we often overestimate our ability to endure. Because of our concern, we believe that we can go on forever. We think that we can be superhuman, losing sight of the fact that we need to be refreshed.

What do you do to relax? Is it difficult for you to give yourself permission to take care of yourself in the midst of helping? Why? Can you see why this is important?

Once I worked with a woman whose husband called her a "sprinter." He told her that she could run hard and fast for about six weeks. Then she would lose steam quickly. His insight was valuable as she learned to set her pace for helping. She realized that she was more effective in short-term crises than in chronic circumstances that would tap her resources for long periods of time.

At that point, she was helping a young mother in her book club whose son had leukemia. She was exhausted, so she suggested that they call on some other women in their church to take her place for a while. Several women offered to oversee her responsibilities for a few days.

When she realized that she was free to take time for herself, she exclaimed, "I wish I could get on a big boat and take a cruise somewhere!" She could not afford a cruise, but she bought a worship CD, a journal, bubble bath, a scented candle and chocolate, and made an appointment for a massage. For two days, she doted on herself. By "taking herself away," she became refreshed and able to see things clearly again. She no longer felt drained because she had given herself time to be filled up. In addition, when she began her helping role again, she continued to involve women from the church as helpers.

If we are going to be able to see someone through a difficulty, we must come to terms with our own humanity and treat ourselves well.

And here are two more points to keep in mind as part of this "prescription." First, we must reserve time to spend with Jesus, just as Jesus reserved time to spend alone with His father. It is wise to do this each day. Second, we need to seek the prayers of others. Without breaking the confidentiality of the person you are helping, ask your friends to pray for you. If your own needs are covered with prayer, you will feel freer to focus on the needs of someone else.

Helping Someone Else Persevere

Now you have the tools you need to persevere through times of potential burnout. With this awareness, you will likely discover that the person you are helping needs perseverance skills as well. Just as the helper needs rest to eradicate burnout, so does the one being helped.

When I meet a troubled person, one of my first goals is to measure his or her hope level. The following comments, for instance, reveal that a person's perseverance level is dangerously low:

"I feel as if this will never stop."
"I just want it to be over."
"I don't think I can live through this."
"God doesn't care."

71

"I can't do it."

"I guess I deserved this."

"It won't ever be any different."

"It's more than I can bear."

Years ago I heard a story of a man who was fishing in the Gulf when his boat capsized. For hours he was able to tread water, watching for another fisherman to come by. Near sundown, nobody had come and he was exhausted.

Suddenly he saw a small plane flying over. He felt a great surge of energy and began to yell and wave his arms. The plane flew by. Immediately his strength evaporated. Just as he was about to give up and go under, he saw a boat on the horizon. His energy surged again, enabling him to wave and yell. Unfortunately the driver of the boat turned in the opposite direction without seeing him. Dejected, he found himself about to sink beneath the waves one more time.

Can you recall a time when you desperately needed hope? Did someone encourage you? What did he/she say to you? What effect did those words have? If there was no one to help you, were you able to encourage yourself? If so, how did you do it?

Just as he was about to succumb to his exhaustion, he saw another boat coming his way. Once again, energy surged within him and he began to wave his arms and yell. The driver of the boat saw him and came to his rescue. The energy and adrenalin he received each time he saw a possible rescue enabled him to hang on until he was found.

Someone may feel that he is drowning in life, sinking beneath the waves of hopelessness. An encouraging word or event can give a surge of energy. Hope is necessary for survival. Hope creates endurance power.

Ways to Offer Hope

There are numerous ways to offer hope to someone who needs to persevere. Some of them may sound familiar to you, such as: sharing a similar story with a good outcome; reading about faith and hope in God's Word; recalling God's faithfulness. Here are several other ways to help someone hang on with hope.

Avoid nostalgia.

When we are going through trials, it is easy to look back and wish for "the good old days." That is what King Solomon envisioned when he said, "Do not say, Why were the old days better than these? For it is not wise or because of wisdom that you ask this" (Ecclesiastes 7:10). We cannot look backward and move forward at the same time.

Several years ago when I was wishing for "better days," a friend said, "Nostalgia is not your friend. In this case, it is your stumbling block." She was right. I was walking into a trap that had no way out.

During his trials, Job fell into the trap of nostalgia, too. He said:

Oh, that I were as in the months of old, as in the days when God watched over me; when His lamp shone above and upon my head, and by His light I walked through darkness . . . when the Almighty was yet with me, and my children were about me; when my steps [through rich pasturage] were washed with butter, and the rock poured out for me streams of oil! When I went out to

He focused on what had been.

the gate of the city, when I prepared my seat in the street—the broad place [for the council at the city's gate]; the young men saw me, and hid themselves; the aged rose up and stood.

Job 29:2–3, 5–8

Job focused on what had been. His hope was gone. Encourage those who long for the past to think forward.

Explain the need for "protection" during vulnerable times.

There are times when people in need must stay away from particular places and people. There are times of the day or night when they may be vulnerable and let hope slip away. You might encourage your friend to have a protection plan for those times, places and people.

Have you or someone you love ever become stuck in nostalgia? What was the effect? How was your experience harmful? Was your progress delayed?

Judy's fiancé broke their engagement. Heartbroken, she drove past his house every evening around ten o'clock to see if his new girlfriend was there. If her car was there, Judy would cry and call him on the phone. He would respond with angry words and tell her never to call again, and she would experience fresh rejection. Then Judy would drive home and play "their" song until she fell asleep. She was not only prolonging her grief but creating fresh grief each day.

Judy had to decide to stop driving by his house so that her broken heart could heal. She agreed to call a friend in the evenings at ten o'clock instead of allowing her mind to turn to her ex-fiancé.

Familiar times of day, people, places—even sounds and smells—can draw us back emotionally into the past. To move forward, your friend will have to leave many of them behind.

Watch for self-pity.

Anyone who looks back and wishes for former, better days will begin to feel as if he should not have to go through hard times. He may begin to justify himself, as if to prove that he is too important to suffer.

Look at Job's self-justification:

I delivered the poor who cried, the fatherless and him who had none to help him. The blessing of him who was about to perish came upon me, and I caused the widow's heart to sing for joy. I put on righteousness, and it clothed me . . . my justice was like a robe and . . . a crown! I was eyes to the blind, and feet was I to the lame. I was a father to the poor and needy.

Have you ever experienced self-pity? If you have, how did you know? What did you do?

Job 29:12–16

Direct the person you are helping away from self-pity. Instead, turn the focus toward God's goodness, His mercy and His many blessings.

Guide your friend away from discouraging people.

Most of us have a family member or a friend who "awfulizes" everything. We know who they are, and when we want comfort, we seek them out. After we spend a short time with them, we are convinced that the problem is even more awful than we thought it was!

This category also includes those people who can sympathize with someone's sorrows, but they cannot be glad for anyone's successes. They temper joy with warnings such as:

> *Can you recall words that some one spoke that drained away your hope? What were they?*

"Don't get too excited. This may not last."

"It may be better today, but tomorrow will be different."

"It's not over yet!"

"Don't get your hopes up too high."

People who discourage are enemies to progress. They drain hope and make efforts toward change appear meaningless. Show your friend how to recognize the discouraging people in her life. Encourage her to avoid them during times of stress.

Encourage self-nurturing.

Set a good example of taking care of yourself and encourage the person you are helping to do the same. Ask good questions:

"In what ways did you relax before this crisis happened?"

"When was the last time you read a good book?"

"Are you eating nourishing meals?"

"Could you sit in the sunshine for a little while?"

On one of your meeting days, suggest that you simply take time off and go to a movie, walk in the park or browse through a bookstore. Find simple things to do together that the person did before the problem began.

Perseverance is possible, provided you and your friend make the effort to give yourselves the care you both need. No one can work continuously and still bear fruit. Even music has rest stops. Nature does also. We must allow seasons of rest so that our strength can be renewed. Then we can continue to make progress.

Before you begin helping another person, make a commitment to yourself. Acknowledge the wisdom in caring for yourself before you try to care for other people. If you will do this, you will be able to persevere through difficult times with those who are suffering and help them do the same.

FIVE

HOW TO HELP SOMEONE WHO IS GRIEVING

On September 11, 2001, as I was leaving the house to meet with my weekly growth group, the phone rang. One of the group members said, "Lynda, turn on CNN! Our country is under attack!"

Her words made no sense to me. Under attack? What did that mean? As I hurried toward the television set, I tried to form a mental picture of our country under attack. I could only imagine troops and tanks and military jets.

A picture came on the television set of two huge buildings collapsing into an enormous pile of concrete and rubble and dust. Smoke was pouring out from the top. As I listened, the announcer explained that jet airliners had crashed into both buildings of the World Trade Center and estimated that many thousands of people had been killed.

79

I watched for a few moments, glanced at my watch and realized that I was almost late for the meeting. As I drove, I felt as if I were in a dream. Nothing seemed real. I was aware that something absolutely horrible had happened, but I could not connect my mind with my emotions. I felt nothing.

Have you ever heard bad news and felt as if you could not connect with your emotions? As if your mind felt jammed? What had happened to put you in that state? Have you ever observed that type of reaction in other people?

When I arrived, several members of our group were seated and staring at the television set. They did not seem to realize that I had entered the room. Others arrived soon after I did, and they appeared to be in a daze.

We watched the news reports for some time, and then I suggested that we go into the meeting room and pray. Although we all bowed our heads, it seemed almost impossible for anyone to formulate a prayer. All mental systems seemed to be jammed.

Stages of Grief

Many different circumstances can precede grief, and there are times when people may experience grief from several different sources all at once. Here are some common causes:

The death of a close relative or friend
A divorce
A move
A broken relationship

80

A job change
A church change
The loss of a job
The loss of health
The death of a pet
The stress of health problems
The loss of personal property
The loss of position
A child leaving home
A lost opportunity

An individual suffering from these or other experiences will usually go through several stages of grief. These stages do not follow any order. Unpredictable and confusing, they can leave the grieving person wondering how he got from one emotional state to another and then back to a previous state again. Many of us are aware of the contributions Elizabeth Kubler-Ross has made in this area of the emotional seesaw of grief.

The First Stage: Shock and Denial

I, as well as the members of the group, was shocked as we met together that morning. One woman commented, "I know this is happening, but it just doesn't seem real. How could it be?" Another one added, "I feel as if I'm in a bad dream and will wake up in a minute."

The emotional numbness that we all felt was a gift from God. It protected us from having to face the reality faster than we were able. We could function in order to do what was required of us, but our feelings were almost completely shut down.

I have witnessed this many times. One evening, for instance, a man called me because he was concerned

81

about his sister. That afternoon she had received a telephone call informing her that her son had been killed in a car wreck. Neighbors went with her to the emergency room and helped her take care of many arrangements that had to be made. As members of the family gathered in her home that evening, she went into the kitchen and began to prepare supper just as she had done every night previously.

As she began to busy herself, her husband said to her, "Honey, people have brought supper. You don't need to do anything. Just sit down and rest." The more he insisted that she rest, however, the stronger her desire became to prepare supper. Finally, the entire family allowed her to cook supper, serve it and clean up the kitchen. There seemed to be nothing else to do!

When our lives have changed drastically, we strive to find ways to keep hold of something familiar. We make an extreme effort to keep things as they were before. That

Why do you think the mother needed to continue her nightly routine, even after her son had been killed? Have you known anyone who behaved this way?

family did the right thing. They gave the mother the freedom to maintain everything she could at the moment except her son. In time, she would begin to be able to face reality for herself, but not then.

If someone you know has experienced a shock, just be with her and let her find her own way back to her emotions.

It is not helpful to attempt to force reality on someone who is in shock. There are, however, times when a physical touch helps. You might carefully reach out and touch the individual, reminding her that she is not alone, but that is enough. Let her remain in the safe place that she has been able to maintain for herself.

The Second Stage: Anger and Fear

As grieved persons begin to connect emotionally with reality, most feel anger over their losses and fear about the future.

For instance, in interviews shown on TV a week or so after the attacks, I began to notice expressions of anger and outrage in people who were close to the damaged area. One man said, "How could this have happened? We'll track those killers down and give them what they deserve. I hope they burn in hell!"

A man who was wandering near the wreckage, carrying signs with pictures of his loved one, cried, "I don't know how I can live without him! He was my brother!"

One newscaster was angry with the government. "Why weren't we prepared for this? How could a country like the United States have been so unaware that this could happen? How could we have been so unprotected?"

Have you ever felt angry over a loss? If you have, did you want someone to pay? Were you afraid that you absolutely could not live without a particular person in your life? How did the people around you react?

A survivor was angry at her situation. "Why should I have lived and my friend died?" She probably was not really angry that she had lived but instead was angry because she had lost her friend.

Often believers do not want to allow another believer to react in anger because they believe that all anger is wrong. (We will discuss anger more fully in chapter 7.) Because of this, they attempt to reason away the anger, minimize the grieving person's pain or actually forbid anger to be expressed. Anger is a normal part of grieving.

For example, I have a friend who lost her job when her company downsized. She had invested her time and effort in that company for years and felt that it was unfair for her to be let go when others who had less experience and expertise were not released. She knew that she would miss having contact with business associates and, of course, she faced the loss of her paycheck as well as a future that looked uncertain.

As she was expressing her thoughts, her sister said, "Well, I think you ought to be more thankful than that! At least you had a good job for a long time. Some people never have a job like that or earn the amount of money you've earned. Remember, you have a lot of investments, so you have no right to be angry!"

Have you ever been with someone who was expressing anger or fear over a loss? Could you understand why he or she felt that way? How did you respond?

Her sister did not know that anger is a normal reaction during the grieving process, and she did not discern the fear that my friend was facing, either.

These feelings can be so intense that grieving persons often feel as if they are going crazy. In fact, anger may be an attempt to convince themselves that there is something they can do to change what has happened. When they find out that they cannot change anything, they often become depressed.

The Third Stage: Depression

No one can remain angry forever. The mind and body cannot sustain the intense emotion, and they begin to let down. Approximately a month after the attacks, I read this newspaper headline: "America Is Depressed." Although most people were not clinically depressed,

84

there was a feeling of sadness that was woven through our lives. Almost no one was untouched by the losses that had occurred. People were getting sick with minor illnesses, missing work, eating more junk food and staying at home by the fire. We were seeking comfort because our emotions were spent.

The Final Stage: Acceptance

As the days pass, reality settles in and the grieving person begins to see that she will be able to go on. Often the question is not "Will I survive this?" but "What should I do now? How do I go on? How can I make a new life?"

The answers may come slowly. Thus, it is not wise to encourage anyone to rush into making decisions soon after they have experienced a great loss. Judgment may be clouded by emotion, driving someone forward in an unwise direction. There is such a great need to reestablish life that many people often make bad mistakes during an adjustment stage, which causes them even more grief later on. It is helpful to encourage grieving people to wait and allow as much time as possible before taking significant steps.

What practical methods do you use to seek comfort when you need it? Can you accept your need for comfort during times of grief and be compassionate toward yourself or do you deny yourself comfort? How do you usually treat others who are grieving?

For example, a man named Joe missed his wife terribly after she died following a prolonged season of illness. After her death he commented, "I grieved a lot while she was sick. I think I faced her death even before she died. I think I'm ready to go on with life. I'm so tired of feeling alone."

Soon, he began to date his deceased wife's best friend. While his wife was alive, people had often commented on the similarities between the two women. Joe married again six months after his wife's death. In many ways, he felt as if he had his wife back again. His new wife had shared recipes with his deceased wife, so she cooked many of the same foods. They soon merged into his familiar circle of old friends as a couple. He was no longer alone.

As the months passed, however, her children began to resent their marriage and did all they could to harm their relationship. Joe and his new wife disagreed on finances. Tensions mounted. Before the year was out, they both declared that the marriage had been a mistake, and she filed for divorce.

Can you see why it is important to delay big decisions until the season of intense grieving is over? Have you or has someone you know reacted hastily after a time of loss? What was the result?

She summed up their experience by saying to Joe, "Marrying you was a way that I felt I could keep my best friend. I should have just given myself time to accept the fact that she is gone and I will not be with her again until I go to heaven. I think you did the same thing. I was so much like your wife that you felt as if you had her back with you. Neither of us faced reality and built a new life. Instead, we just renovated the old life, and it's not going to work."

It also did not work when an attractive woman in her late sixties decided to sell her home and move to a retirement community in Florida after her husband died.

After she arrived, she realized what an uprooting she had experienced. Almost nothing in her life was the same. She felt as if she had lost all of her bearings. Within the year, she sold her home in Florida and returned to the neighborhood where she and her deceased husband had lived. She rejoined the same church, played Tuesday night Bingo again and resumed much of her previous lifestyle.

Life really does go on after a loss, but it goes on more smoothly if wise decisions are made. You might encourage someone who is grieving to seek help from experts in various areas of life, such as finances, real estate or legal matters. Remember, "In the multitude of counselors there is safety" (Proverbs 11:14). When someone is recovering, help him see the value of input from those he respects.

Why People Get Stuck in Grief

Sometimes people get stuck in the stages of grief and are not able to move on to acceptance and closure. When this happens, their suffering is prolonged. Here are some of the reasons people get stuck.

Frozen Feelings

Some people will not allow themselves to grieve. They are afraid that if they let themselves feel grief, they will be totally overcome by the intensity of loss. They are afraid that they will drop into a deep, dark emotional hole and never come up again. They fear ultimate destruction by grief.

It is helpful to know that grief usually comes in waves that last approximately twenty to thirty minutes. Our bodies and minds cannot endure extreme intensity longer than that. Once the limit is reached, there is then a plateau.

Expressing grief is healthy because it allows relief from pain and stress, giving time for the body and mind to regain strength. When someone knows that there is a limit to the next wave of grief, it is not as frightening to let himself feel.

Unresolved Guilt and Regrets

When we lose a person, a job, or a way of life, it is natural to look back and try to find ways you wish you had "done it better." Of course, we will all find times when we said or did the wrong thing, failed to grasp an opportunity or made a careless, costly decision. The problem arises when someone gets stuck in guilt and regret and does not understand how to receive God's grace so that she can gradually adjust and continue with her life.

For example, the small son of a friend of mine was killed when he rode his scooter down the driveway and out into the street in front of a car. He had been forbidden to ride his scooter past the garage, but, in his enthusiasm, he rode past the boundaries that his mother had set. After his death she cried, "I should never have bought that scooter! I knew it could be dangerous, but he wanted it so badly. I gave in when I shouldn't have! It's all my fault!"

Have you ever blamed yourself for a grievous event? Have you known someone else who did? What were the circumstances?

It is impossible for us to foresee every potential for danger, evaluate it correctly and protect everyone we know. There is a lot of built-in risk in just being alive on this earth.

My friend finally came to terms with the fact that she did not have control over the life of her child at every moment. As is common with children, her son had decided to disobey his mother, and his choice had resulted in his death. When my friend faced reality, her grief did not decrease, but she was able to find release from blame.

Fear of Forgetting

Sometimes we resist letting go of someone or something in life because we are afraid that we will forget. This resistance may be accompanied by exaggerated feelings of loyalty.

Moving on will not cause us to forget. It may, however, distance us from the memories and feelings. This is actually beneficial because we cannot live in the past and the present at the same time. You can help a grieving friend set appropriate times at which he can choose to remember, such as certain holidays or birthdays or anniversaries. When specific times are set to remember, there will be less fear of forgetting and your friend will be more likely to give himself permission to move forward in his life.

Loss of Attention

When someone is in a crisis or experiences a loss, her support system goes into action. The grieving person may be reluctant to give up this extra attention.

An elderly woman named Emma said, "Everyone is so worried about me now that my husband has died. I think I'll be okay, but I don't want to be alone. I'm afraid that if people see me doing well, they'll forget about me. Am I using my grief to bind people to me? Would they really come back if I did well?"

Self-pity versus Gratitude

It is hard to accept loss and move on in life if we are not thankful. It is just too easy to get mad and feel sorry for ourselves. When we do that, it is as if we are driving with one foot on the gas and the other foot on the brake. We will have false starts and stops, but we will make no progress.

The person you are helping may find it difficult to begin to count his blessings after a loss, but it is necessary. Self-pity is a powerful negative emotion that can take root quickly and become a way of life. I once heard a pastor say, "Self-pity is just a step away from insanity or death." I think he was probably right.

Be careful how you encourage your grieving friend away from self-pity. It is not helpful, for instance, to say, "But you still have so much to be thankful for." Rather, try this: "I know this is such a hard time. Does it help you to remember some of the good times? Would you like to tell me about those?" If he will do that, you can point out that the same God who blessed him in the past will bless him in different ways in the future. You might also ask, "How would you like for God to bless you now?" As he sees God answer his prayers, his gratitude will increase.

Questioning: Why, God, Why?

Many things happen that we do not understand. Because we have a human need to make sense of our circumstances, we ask *Why?* Perhaps we believe that if we can understand *how* something happened, we can prevent it from happening again. We try to find some power over our circumstances in order to feel safe.

It is all right to ask God for answers. We need to be careful, however, that if He does not provide explanations we do not assign motives and actions to God that may be inaccurate.

After the attacks, for example, I heard several people say, "This is God's wake-up call to America!" Others said, "It's God's judgment!" Those perceptions may be accurate, but they also may not be. The attacks could simply have been the result of an evil plan that God allowed because the terrorists had free will.

Have you or someone you know been stuck in grief? Why do you think this happened? Can you see ways that this could have been avoided?

Similarly, others believe: "God paid me back for my unconfessed sins" or "God finally gave me what I deserve." Caution someone who is grieving not to attempt to formulate reasons and assign them to God. God will reveal what we need to know.

Giving Comfort to the Grieving

There are many simple ways to offer comfort. Some of them are:

*A **listening ear***—Sometimes it helps people recover from grief to express feelings and memories until they are "done." A year ago a friend named Jamie was raped. She needed to talk about that night for months, and gradually she diffused most of the pain of the memory.

God's Word—Choose Scriptures of comfort and hope for the future. Ask the grieving person to read them with you.

Music—Music can be uplifting. A tape or CD that includes praise music is a great gift to someone who is grieving. Words of Scripture can fill the soul of a grieving person when he does not have the energy or focus to read. Classical music can be restful. Nostalgic selections are not usually helpful because they take the grieving one back into the past and may get him stuck again.

A note in the mail—In an age of e-mail and answering machines, a handwritten note is a concrete symbol of love. A friend of mine bought a dozen note cards, wrote a loving note plus a Bible verse on each one and mailed one a week to her aunt after her daughter died.

Noting special anniversaries—Some people dread anniversaries of special times. They fear the grief and feelings of loneliness that might erupt. Offering to spend time with them on those occasions can dilute the fear and carry them over.

Gifts in memory—Giving a monetary gift to a charity or worthy cause is an effective way to offer comfort to someone who is grieving. It shows appreciation for the contributions or interests of the person who is gone.

Flowers—Even though someone is grieving, the sight of a flower can be a symbol of love. Flowers can stimulate a happy feeling that may surprise even the grieving one.

Warm blankets or quilts—I heard a report that people were buying blankets and afghans after the attacks of September 11. People wanted to wrap up, get cozy, feel warm and protected. Sometimes the gift of a blanket or afghan is comforting and is a change from the usual remembrances.

Nature—Nature brings most of us closer to God. Romans tells us that we can sense His presence in nature. Sunshine makes almost anyone feel better!

Nature also reminds us that all of life has beginnings and endings, seasons to be enjoyed and seasons to let go, and then it starts all over again.

I once saw a cemetery beside a country church. There were beautiful flowering trees in the churchyard, as well as in the cemetery. That scene was a vivid picture of life, death and eternity. Life never really ends. It just changes. We relocate and we meet again.

As you are sensitive to the Lord's leading, you will undoubtedly find many ways to express your love and concern to someone who is overcome by grief. Here are a few verses to guide you and to share with the one you are helping.

Scriptures for Meditation

Psalm 119:50
Isaiah 49:13
Isaiah 61:1–3
Matthew 5:4
1 Corinthians 15:55–57
2 Corinthians 1:3–4
2 Thessalonians 2:16–17
Hebrews 4:15–16
Revelation 21:4

SIX

HOW TO HELP SOMEONE WHO IS SICK

Last spring, when Nancy began having difficulty breathing, she was diagnosed with asthma. Several days later, her physician called. He had just read her chest scan from a few days before and discovered a mass in her left lung!

Nancy exclaimed to me, "I felt immediate anxiety, wondering if *mass* was a medical code word for *cancer*. I couldn't see how this could have happened! I have never smoked and I've always been so healthy. My doctor's news made no sense!"

Like Nancy, when we get bad news most of us cannot grasp the full impact immediately. It takes time for our minds to process the facts and incorporate them into our lives. Even a person with strong faith needs some time to process and find his or her balance. When you are helping someone who has just found out that he might be seriously ill, remember to allow time for him to face the truth in his own way. The concerns that each person has will be different.

Nancy's concerns focused on a change in lifestyle. "Believe it or not, my greatest fear initially was not of dying. I am a Type-A personality," she explained, "and one of my greatest concerns was the realization that for some time I would be physically incapable of performing the routine tasks of cooking for my family, taking care of my home, even running errands. I realized that I would have to depend on others, and I imagined myself sitting around, feeling helpless and unproductive."

Have you ever had a serious illness? If you have, what was your first reaction?

Each person has to come to terms with the realities of his circumstances in a different way. During this time, your presence is invaluable. (See chapter 1.)

Common Questions of Those Facing Sickness

People who are sick may have many questions. Here are some of the most common.

If I pray and then rely on medical science, does it mean I don't have enough faith? Doesn't God care enough to answer my prayer?

When Nancy learned about the mass in her chest—later defined as a malignant tumor—she, as well as many friends, began to pray for her healing. She said, "Each day I took several deep breaths to see if my breathing had become any easier, just knowing that the tumor was gradually disappearing. I was scheduled for surgery and even as we drove to the hospital, I believed that God would heal me at the last minute. But God had a greater healing in mind for me.

"When I entered the ICU waiting area, I saw about twenty-five people interceding for me. I could not believe that many people would actually come to the hospital!

"Upon examination, the surgeon found that the tumor was still there. Once the operation began, he saw that it was malignant. He was forced to remove the upper left lobe of my lung, hoping to contain the spread of the cancer.

"When I came out of ICU, people came into my hospital room and stood around my bed and prayed for me. They sang songs of praise. Later, during my recovery, I could not believe how many people came to my aid. They brought food for my family, ran errands, sent cards and called often. The outpouring of love I received astounded me! Every need I had was met. It was as if Jesus was telling me how much He loved me through each set of eyes that smiled at me. I would have missed out on this extended blessing of receiving God's love if I had been instantly, supernaturally healed. God had a surprise for me! He not only delivered me from disease, but He changed my heart forever through the love of the helpers

> *After prayer, have you ever felt uncertain about using medication? Did you wonder if you lacked faith in God?*

He sent to me. He gave me what I needed the most.

"I learned that God's love is realized most deeply through our personal experiences in life. God performed a miraculous healing for me and He used surgery, medications and people to heal my mind, body and spirit."

Nancy discovered a comfortable balance between prayers of faith for healing and letting God work through medical science. If the person you are helping worries about this issue, remind her that our creative Father has many avenues of healing. Only He knows how to combine those various methods in the ways that will not only heal her body but increase wholeness in her entire being.

Remind her that everything that God has made is good. Substances that help the body heal, as well as physicians who serve and people who mend hearts with their love have all been created by God.

Review James 1:17, which says, "Every good gift and every perfect (free, large, full) gift is from above; it comes down from the Father." Encourage your friend to receive every good gift!

Am I being punished?

A single young woman named Sally contracted a sexually transmitted disease when she had an affair with a married man. She felt that her sickness was punishment from God. Failing to understand God's mercy and forgiveness, she believed that she would now be in pain forever.

Psalm 119:67 says, "Before I was afflicted I went astray, but now Your word do I keep [hearing, receiving, loving and obeying it]." Although Sally's sickness was directly connected to her sin, she had repented and no longer needed to fear punishment. While there were consequences for her behavior, she was able to understand that God had forgiven her and would guide her as she sought treatment.

If you are helping a sick person who believes that her illness is a punishment to be endured, study Scriptures such as James 5:13–16 and Psalm 103:3.

And remember, just because our sicknesses are sometimes preceded by our sins, we need to be careful not to attribute every sickness to sin. We live in a fallen world. The environment is often unhealthy. We breathe air that is not clean and eat foods that may be contaminated by poisons or may not be properly cooked. We may have inherited a genetic physical weakness. Sickness can come from various sources.

If you are communicating with someone who is sick, be sure to look at the big picture and avoid making assumptions. If your friend has questions about the cause of her illness, encourage her to take her concerns to God in prayer.

Does God want me to be well? What is His will?

In my previous book, *An Invitation to Healing*, I related how a friend asked me an important question when I was facing a time of personal illness: "Do you believe it is God's will for you to get well?" Because I could not give a knowledgeable, confident answer, I began an intensive Scripture search to find God's will about healing. I had been in severe pain for a long time and during the times when I became ambivalent, my faith and strength had been drained. I felt confused. I knew that I would not be able to persevere through the healing process unless my faith was firmly established. As I studied God's Word, I asked the Holy Spirit to teach me.

I began my search in the Old Testament where God introduced Himself as our Healer. Speaking to Moses and the Israelites, He introduced Himself as Healer, saying, "for I am the Lord Who heals you" (Exod. 15:26).

I immediately became God's patient, submitting to Him in mind, body and spirit. He became my primary physician.

As my studies began in the New Testament, I discovered in the eighth chapter of Matthew that Jesus healed a leper, a paralyzed servant and Peter's mother-in-law. He freed people who were bound by demonic spirits. Following those accounts were these words:

> And thus He fulfilled what was spoken by the prophet Isaiah, He Himself took (in order to carry away) our weaknesses and infirmities and *bore away our diseases.*
>
> Matthew 8:17, emphasis added

I realized that Jesus had been sent to carry out God's will for people who were sick. In fact, He spent approximately one-third of His ministry healing people!

In His mercy, Jesus never turned anyone away because the disease was too serious (for example, the case of the leper told in Matthew 8:2–3) or because the person had been sick for too long (the man at the pool in John 5:5–9) or because of sin (the crippled man in Mark 2:1–12). Jesus healed everyone who came to Him, regardless of the affliction. In doing so He was obeying the will of His Father. He said, "I have come down from heaven, not to do My own will and purpose; but to do the will and purpose of Him Who sent Me" (John 6:38).

Have you ever felt uncertain about God's will? Have you studied Bible verses on healing? What do you believe?

Thus, I realized that not only did Jesus come to save us, He came to heal us, too. As I studied the word *salvation,* I found in *Strong's Concordance* that it means "to deliver, protect, preserve, to heal and make whole."

Although I was saved, I wanted all of the wholeness God had granted me through Jesus. I wanted to be healed!

My faith began to increase every day.

You, too, can encourage the one you are helping to believe in God's will for our healing. Scripture makes it clear that God desires our wholeness. Help your friend to trust in God's incredible love for His children.

Why isn't everyone healed?

I do not know the answer to that question. I do not know anyone who does. I do know, however, that it is a mistake to base our own faith on someone else's experience. The only valid basis for faith and truth is God's Word.

We are told to walk by faith and not by sight (see Hebrews 11:1). If we base our faith on what we have seen in the lives of other people, we will become confused. We will be living *their* experiences instead of drawing near to God and living out our *own* processes of healing.

Encourage your friend to learn from God's Word, not base his knowledge on someone else's life. Help him to focus in particular on knowing Him through His Word.

Paul said, "[For my determined purpose is] that I may know Him—that I may progressively become more deeply and intimately acquainted with Him, perceiving and recognizing and understanding [the wonders of His Person] more strongly and more clearly" (Philippians 3:10).

The best is always ahead for those who know Him. When we reach heaven, we will marvel at His mercy. And all pain and suffering will cease forever (see Revelation 21:4).

What about Paul's thorn?

This is a common question. Bible scholars have pondered Paul's condition. The "thorn" is identified as a "messenger of Satan" (2 Corinthians 12:7). Some commentators believe that his affliction was the constant persecution he endured. Some believe that it was an ongoing temptation. Others have decided that he had an eye condition or some other physical ailment.

Whether Paul's pain was physical, emotional, spiritual or circumstantial, he had some type of condition from which he wanted to be released. However, as I studied his life, I found that he was able to travel, to preach, to do miracles, to perform signs and wonders, to endure prison and to write a great portion of the New Testament! Paul said, "When I am weak (in human strength), then am I [truly] strong—able, powerful in divine strength. . . . For *I have not fallen short one bit or proved myself at all inferior*" (2 Corinthians 12:10–11, emphasis added).

Paul was not lacking in anything that he really needed to fulfill his purpose. Paul was surrendered to God's will for his life, drawing on Him constantly, but never coming up short. That is what we all need.

> *Have you ever based your outlook on the experience of someone else? Has doing that been a stumbling block for you? Has it blocked your own vision?*

Do I really want to be well?

We may wonder about God's will concerning our healing, but Jesus asks a similar question of us. Think of the man at the pool of Bethesda (see John 5:2–9). He had been lingering there, suffering, for 38 years. Just imagine what a change healing would bring to his life!

He would have to become responsible not only for himself but also for others. He would no longer be the focus of those around him. Jesus asked, "Do you want to become well? [Are you really in earnest about getting well?]"

Although we may think *Of course I want to be well!* we need to reflect upon the question that Jesus proposed. We need to recognize that there are things that God promises to do, and there are things God requires of us. Healing is a process. Obedience is often required for release of emotional or physical bondage.

Some areas where obedience may be required in order for healing to be received are:

Confessing sin and releasing guilt (Proverbs 28:13; Romans 6:11–14; Hebrews 4:14–16; James 5:13–16)

Forgiving self and others (Mark 2:1–12)

Releasing shame and self-condemnation (Isaiah 43:25; 54:4; 61:7; John 5:24; Romans 8:1)

Giving up harmful habits (Isaiah 55:7; Ephesians 4:22–24; James 4:17)

Being willing to take responsibility again (John 5:2–9)

Giving up attention-getting mechanisms (Matthew 10:38; Ephesians 4:29; 5:4–9)

Total surrender is the fastest way to receive healing for your mind, body and spirit.

Why We Can Pray in Faith

God desires our wholeness—body, mind and spirit. Not only did He make this possible through the sacrifice of His Son, but He continues to give us encouragement and comfort through the Holy Spirit. Let's take a moment to look at these extraordinary concepts.

The Ministry of the Holy Spirit

The Holy Spirit, the third Person of the Trinity, is God with us on the earth today. Jesus, who now sits enthroned at the right hand of God, has sent the Holy Spirit—the Helper—as promised (see John 16:7–8; Acts 1:5; 2:32–33, 38–39).

While I was sick, I spent many hours in the offices of physicians waiting to be seen. I finally realized that the Holy Spirit was with me all the time! I did not have to wait for an appointment or be put on a list to be called when He was available. I began to draw on His comfort, strength and healing power. He progressively delivered me from fear, giving me peace and helping my body relax.

First Corinthians 12 tells us that when the Holy Spirit was poured out, God gave special gifts to all believers, including the gift of healing. When we pray for the sick, the Holy Spirit is carrying out the will of the Father through our prayers.

The Healing Power in the Blood of Jesus

One of my favorite movies is the classic *Ben Hur*. If you have seen this movie, you probably remember one of the last scenes when three women sought shelter from the storm after the Crucifixion. Two of the women had arrived too late to receive their healing from Jesus. Disappointed, they had run into a cave when the thunder and lightning began. Do you recall seeing the blood of Jesus pouring down from His body as He hung on the cross? Do you recall the astonishment of the two lep-

104

rous women when they saw that they were healed as the blood began to flow? Do you recall their wonder and joy?

This scene presents a graphic picture of the spiritual reality that we may experience today if we understand the entire purpose of the cross: Jesus' death secured not only our salvation but our healing as well.

Throughout history, many heroes have suffered and died for us, but the suffering of Jesus accomplished something for sinful humanity that no one else on earth could ever hope to achieve. Not only did Jesus suffer physical pain and death, but He also bore on His own body the sins of everyone who had ever lived and ever would live.

The blood of Jesus is unique. First Peter 1:19 refers to it as "precious blood . . . like that of a [sacrificial] lamb without blemish or spot."

Have you ever thought about the fact that the blood of Jesus flowed through the body of someone who never had an evil thought? The effects of toxic emotions, such as bitterness and resentment, never contaminated His body. His mind was filled with the peace of God. He never experienced guilt or fear. His blood is the only substance pure enough to cleanse our sins and to obtain wholeness for us.

Hebrews 9:12 says, "He went once for all into the [Holy of] Holies [of heaven], not by virtue of the blood of goats and calves . . . but His own blood, having found and secured a complete redemption—an everlasting release [for us.]"

No other human being ever has—or could—do that for us. The "exchanges" of the cross make true release possible. Because of His blood, it is possible to exchange sickness for health, weakness for His strength, distress for peace, sorrow for joy, and guilt for cleansing and forgiveness.

If you are helping someone who does not believe that healing is included as one of the blessings of the cross, don't make it a point of argument. Simply remind the person that God hears and answers our prayers, no matter what we may bring to Him.

Throughout Scripture, the Father, Jesus and the Holy Spirit performed healing. They continue to work in agreement with one another in our lives today.

You might want to encourage the one you are helping to pursue the following avenues of healing in addition to medical science:

Laying on of hands and prayer (Mark 6:5; 7:32–35; 16:18)

Anointing with oil (James 5:14–15)

Praying in the authority of His name (John 16:23; Acts 4:7, 10; Philippians 2:9–10)

Prayers of spiritual warfare and deliverance (Matthew 10:8; Luke 13:11–16; John 10:10; Acts 5:16)

Laughter (Proverbs 17:22)

In addition, suggest that your friend study the healing stories found in the Old and New Testaments. During the process, much wisdom and knowledge can be gained that may not only lead to healing for the sick person but also equip him or her to become an agent of healing in the future.

A Faith-Building "Tip List"

In *An Invitation to Healing* I told the story of Bill, a man who battled prostate cancer for six years. When he was first diagnosed, he was given a 30 percent chance of living for five years. In spite of this, Bill continues to live a dynamic life. For a long period he was cancer-free. The cancer returned, however, and once again he went to Jehovah Rapha and submitted himself for healing. Bill is now in the eighth year of his healing process.

I visited with Bill recently, asking him to make a list of insights that have given him the ability to "live well" while he is suffering. These are his tips for those who are sick.

- *Stay around positive, expectant people.* The other day I was at my doctor's office waiting for my weekly treatment. In the small room were two women who decided to play "I can top that!" with their own stories of cancer. The atmosphere quickly became almost suffocating. I picked up my thick medical file and headed for a chair in the hall. No way! Enough of that! The nurse located me just fine in the hall.

- *Cultivate a positive attitude at the beginning of every day.* I do this by spending time in God's Word, praying and worshipping. I also journal, recording my "thanks you's" from the previous day. This is powerful medicine! At the end of my quiet time, I mark my calendar with the "must do" items for the day. There! I have some "to do's" that are important and I will not be left to wallow in self-pity.

- *Do not own the disease, nor let it own you!* I caught myself speaking to my wife of "my cancer." I said, "Wait a minute. This is not my cancer! I don't want it or anything connected to it. I will not allow it to own me." Words are powerful and must be brought into line with what we really believe.

- *Ministry is daily "work"; plan it in advance.* No matter how I feel, I make my life one of ministry. Giving to others pumps life full of vigor and expectation. Outside of my family, for instance, I mentor young men. God has blessed me in this work, and I learn new things every day.

- *Keep a daily routine.* This is important in living with disease. I pace myself by taking a nap every day after lunch. I know that I will have less energy in the late afternoon and evening so I plan my most energy-intensive work in the morning. Rest is just part of the deal! I have learned not to resent that. My wife fixed up my bed with a down mattress and comforter and great reading lamps. It is a great place for me to enjoy reading before I go to sleep, and I have come to look forward to this pleasure daily.

- *Include some fun in your life pattern.* Our fifteen-year-old daughter is on the "pom" squad at school. We carry a load of girls to all the ballgames. That's fun! I wouldn't trade anything for it. In fact, we have not missed a game. We have built memories never to be forgotten. Sure, cancer and treatments slow me down, but the kids never notice and I have more fun than anyone does!

- *Stay open to new ideas, books, resources and helps that are sent your way.* I have recently been reading books about heaven. This study has transformed my entire expectation of eternity and what happens at death. I have never been so invigorated and blessed. Whether my exit from earth occurs this year or twenty years from now, I see it as the most exciting adventure of all. Live one day at a time. Jesus taught this in Matthew 6:34. Good advice, especially when dealing with a disease.

- *Keep favorite Scriptures hot in the oven of your heart.* Over the years, scores of promises from God's Word have been my "hot ones" at various times. Over the past few months, Psalm 139 has blessed and guided me in a special way, especially verse 16: "Your eyes saw my unformed body. All the days ordained for me were written in your book before one of them came to be" (NIV). What a truth on which to anchor hope! My life span on earth has been predetermined. And my lifespan with my Savior is eternal, already underway. What could be better?

- *Recognize the limits of medicine.* Tests come and go. Statistics are not necessarily dependable in your case. Focus on what you are doing right now. How do you feel? Do what you feel like doing. Forget what the tests say, go ahead. If you need medical attention, by all means get it, but do not be a slave to statistics and test results.

- *Accept God's provision of prayer or help from others.* Two women came into my life this year who have been praying together for people for eighteen years. And they wanted to pray for me! Most weeks they come by for a time of intercession for me. My wife and I have experienced new life from their ministry of prayer. These women believe God!

- *Worship and praise God.* Ephesians 5:20 says to give thanks in all circumstances. Not *for* all circumstances but in the midst of all circumstances.

- *Above all, draw near to Him and know Him.* In Exodus 23:25, God told His people: "Worship the LORD your God, and his blessing will be on your food and water. I will take away sickness from among you. . . . I will give you a full life span" (NIV). Worship Him! Life flows from the Life-Giver to the Worshipper.

Bill hosts Men's Fraternity, a ministry to more than a thousand men at our church. Each week he bounds up onto the platform and ministers in the strength and power of the Holy Spirit who strengthens him every day. As I visited with Bill and read his list of tips, I could see that healing has been given on many different levels over and over. As he says, he is a blessed man!

Carolyn's Miracle

I want to close with the testimony of a woman, Carolyn, who received a miracle. Let this encourage you as you and your friend seek healing.

> Three and a half years ago, I found myself exhausted, anemic and in pain. My energy was gone by the time I forced myself out of bed in the morning.
>
> I visited my physician who recommended that I have a hysterectomy. A few days before surgery, I had a routine abdominal ultrasound so that there would not be any surprises during surgery. As she was concluding the test, the technician said, "You have a cyst on your ovary." She spent more time scanning my right side. I knew that I had just started on a downhill roller-coaster ride.
>
> When I was dressed and heading out the door, she touched me on the arm, looked me in the eye and said, "Carolyn, it's not a cyst." I'll never forget that moment. I had worked in hospitals for 22 years. I've given that kind, sympathetic look to many patients. This time it was for me. All that sympathy was for me.
>
> I had blood tests for signs of cancer and they came back positive. Every sign indicated malignancy. A routine hysterectomy became emergency surgery. When I relayed the news to my husband, Ed, we looked up information on ovarian cancer and I went straight past fear to numbness. Ovarian cancer is aggressive and deadly. Ed immediately began to make plans to take a leave from work. He was sure that he would be burying me.

The night before my surgery, some friends came to pray for me. One friend specifically prayed for God to heal me. When I heard his words, something happened that is difficult for me to describe. A shock wave went through me, and it was as if time had stopped. It was as if I were removed from my friends and in God's presence, talking directly to Him. I realized I had done everything but ask Him to heal me. I was given the ability to ask Him boldly to heal me. I still wasn't sure what the outcome would be, but I had the most incredible peace.

When I lay down that night to sleep, I waited for the familiar pain and exhaustion to wash over me as it always did. It never happened. I had no pain. I slept better that night than I could remember having slept in months.

The next day, as Ed and our pastors and friends waited at the hospital, the mood was

Have you ever known anyone who received a healing miracle? If so, what were the circumstances?

sober, but I felt happy and energized. That is not the normal response to ovarian cancer, and I remember wondering how I could feel so good. I wondered if I were becoming hysterical.

After I had been in surgery for an hour, the phone in the waiting room rang and the surgeon spoke to Ed. The report was simple. It was benign. Ed collapsed to his knees and broke down. He was prepared for "malignant" but not for "benign." What a celebration there was in the waiting room that day! God delivered me from sickness and death. I do not know why He chose to give me such a wonderful miracle. Ed and I are quiet foot soldiers in the Kingdom of God. We sort of get lost in the crowd. We can be easily ignored or overlooked, but God knew exactly where we were, and He performed an instantaneous healing in my body. Blessed be the name of the Lord Jesus Christ!

Scriptures for Meditation

Psalms 103; 107
Proverbs 4:20–23
Isaiah 53:4–5
Jeremiah 17:14, 30.17
Matthew 8; 9:35
Luke 6:19
1 Peter 2:24

SEVEN

HOW TO HELP SOMEONE WHO IS ANGRY

Marla grew up in a home where she was taught that it was not "Christian" to get angry. The skirmishes between her siblings were largely ignored, as were the frequent outbursts of her enraged older sister. Marla never saw her parents have an argument, although she heard raised voices coming from her parents' room late at night. She learned later that they had endured a miserable marriage "because of the children." Since her home *appeared* to be so peaceful, her friends told her how lucky she was. She had agreed.

When Marla went to college and met Clark, she was drawn to him because he seemed so easygoing and agreeable. She felt comfortable with his peaceful exterior because it was familiar, like that of her childhood. She married him and looked forward to having a loving home. Little did she know that just under the surface boiled the same type of anger that was hidden in her parents' home. It did not take long for it to emerge.

Marla was unprepared to deal with Clark's attacks of rage. She did not know how to respond. She had been taught to be submissive to her husband, that he was in charge as the "head of the house." Her desire to be a good Christian, plus her inadequacy to deal with conflict, set her up for abuse from an angry husband.

"I felt ashamed of feeling so angry inside," Marla said. "People told me constantly how lucky I was to have Clark. He didn't drink, smoke or flirt with other women. He made an excellent living and I didn't have to get a job. He was a leader in our church and he read his Bible every day. People loved and admired him.

"I was too embarrassed to talk to anyone about his rages at home, how he would frequently put his fist through the walls, yell at our children and walk out of the room when I tried to talk to him. I felt like a 'non-person' around him. He was the 'head' and I did not believe that I had the right to an opinion. Above all, I was not allowed to be angry. But I was. I had been taught early in life that anger is a sin, however, so I stuffed my anger so far down inside that I hardly knew it was there. Besides, I hated conflict and I enjoyed the illusion of peace, so I complied with his every whim.

"For example, I wouldn't spend money. I made our children's clothes. I clipped coupons for groceries and if I ran out of my allotted amount ahead of time, I would spend enormous amounts of mental energy trying to figure out how to put meals on the table. I would not ask Clark for money because I feared his anger. I gave him complete control over my thoughts, my energy, my emotions and my actions.

"I did this because I believed that it would be wrong for me to 'be angry.' I also wanted to please God and I didn't want Him to be mad at me, either. I let my fear of

Clark and my fear of God cause me to hide my anger, even from myself."

The Overflow of Anger Toward Others

Anger is an intense emotion. Described in the Bible as an "overwhelming flood" (Proverbs 27:4), we see that it is powerful. And it can be unpredictable. Think of anger as a water hose lying in the yard. If you do not grip the handle when you turn on the water full force, the hose will twist and turn and spray water in all directions.

Have you ever been afraid of the impact of someone's anger? Do you know someone who has been afraid of another person for a long time? If so, how did the fear affect her life?

It was no surprise that Marla's anger began to spill out onto others.

Toward Children

Marla explained, "The worst thing my hidden anger caused was my own abuse toward my children whom I loved more than life. I brushed my daughter's hair too hard. I jerked my little one's arm too hard when he accidentally stepped into the street. I raised my voice too loud when reprimanding and I frowned a lot. I had such a heavy weight of negative energy in my soul that I could not be emotionally available to them."

Toward Self

Marla continued, "I felt guilty because my children did not deserve to suffer the consequences of my anger, which I was trying hard to deny and control. As I continued to abuse them, I became more and more angry toward myself. When Clark came home at night, I began to provoke his abuse toward me because I felt as if I deserved it for mistreating our children."

Toward Everyone

Marla said, "When I wasn't blaming myself, my anger suddenly would turn toward Clark, although I worked hard to treat him with what I thought was 're-spect.' I made myself available for his every need. I smiled and complied. I didn't require anything of him because I thought that would be selfish. And deep down in my soul, my hatred of him frightened me. I secretly wished that he would die, leaving me to start over with someone else. This was adultery at its root, and I felt guilty about that, too.

Have you ever been out of control due to anger? Have you ever directed your anger toward innocent people? If so, who were they? How did you feel afterward?

"I resented Christians who seemed to have happy lives and marriages. Secretly I was pleased when something bad happened to them. Then I felt guilty because, as a Christian, I was supposed to love others and pray for their good."

Marla was caught in a vicious trap of anger, guilt and fear.

What Is Anger?

Although we may not realize it, anger is a secondary emotion. Other emotions precede anger, but we are not aware of them because they escalate into anger so quickly.

One emotion that precedes anger is *hurt.* When someone hurts us, we feel the pain, but the need to defend ourselves comes quickly. Anger gives us the energy to defend ourselves.

Fear, as well as *a sense of helplessness,* can also escalate into anger quickly. We may not know how to respond to fear. If we feel the need to escape, our bodies begin to help us by producing energy. Our systems become flooded with adrenaline.

Anger can also be the result of *chronic frustration.* The "last straw" comes, and if our anger goes unchecked we explode. The incident can be insignificant and this response may appear to be irrational and excessive.

For example, Marla was desperate in her marriage. Full of negative feelings, she needed only a little provocation, such as a cup of spilled milk, in order to become angry. The emotional reactions that were always so near the surface would erupt.

We will return to Marla's story in a moment. With her, we will learn that changes can be made. First, however, let's look at the subject of anger. Then I will show you and your friend how to determine if anger is an issue that he or she may want to address.

Understanding Anger

Anger often has roots in childhood trauma. Many adults have been angry since childhood because of verbal, physical or sexual abuse. (See chapter 11 on abuse.) When abused children grow up, their anger erupts. Many children may have had to take over adult responsibilities too early because of the illness or loss of a parent and they had no outlet for their frustrations. They have been angry for so long that they do not even recognize their anger.

People who should protect us often hurt us. Painful or unjust circumstances happen to us even as adults. And when this happens we can become angry with ourselves, others or God.

We become angry when we are rejected, betrayed, embarrassed or overlooked. We can become angry if we get sick or lose a job or if someone we love dies. When we are simply not appreciated, we become angry.

Everyone gets angry, but many deal with anger in unhealthy ways, such as stuffing the anger inside or hurling abuse at others.

The Emotional Range of Anger

Anger exists in degrees. For example, the most intense form of anger is rage. Rage may mean an instantaneous outburst to a new situation or it may simmer as "old anger" that has been stuffed inside for a long time. Regardless, when rage is expressed outwardly, it is easily identified as a form of anger.

Milder forms of anger, such as resentment, bitterness, irritation, agitation and anxiety, are easier to disguise. For example, I was recently visiting with a woman who said, "Of course, I'm not angry! I'm just irritated." However, she was sitting on the edge of her chair, gripping her fists. Her face was flushed. She was laboring to keep her emotions under control, but her body was giving her away.

The Physical Range of Anger

Whether we are aware of it or not, our bodies express our anger and give us clues that we may be getting out of control. For example, when we become angry, our muscles tighten, we may get knots in our stomachs and our blood pressure may go up. Our faces may become flushed, fists clenched. We may find it difficult to sit still. We begin to pace, gesturing, talking in a loud voice. We may speak faster and faster, unable to slow down. If we lose control, we may hit someone. Assault and murder are sometimes the ultimate result of rage.

We may feel ourselves losing control and try to regain it by withdrawing, isolating and pouting. One minute we may want to punish the one who "made us angry" and the next minute, we are angry with ourselves. We may punish ourselves in various ways, and then find false ways to comfort ourselves.

Can you identify the physiological responses of your body during times of anger? If so, what are they? Do you know someone who appears to punish herself? How does she do it?

This was true for Marla. She said, "The anger that I tried too hard to control exposed itself in several ways. I learned that food could be a very effective drug for anger and anxiety, so I ate when I wasn't hungry to calm myself inside. Of course, the extra eating added pounds, and then I didn't like the way I looked. Then I felt guilty about having such little self-control.

"Sometimes my anger would cause me to work feverishly. I moved furniture, mowed the lawn or cleaned obsessively. I volunteered for almost any job at church, often to the neglect of my health, and called it godly sacrifice. I was exhausted all the time. Then I felt guilty for neglecting my children."

Is It Sinful to Be Angry?

Anger is simply an emotion. In its purest form, it is unexpressed energy. Anger does not become sin unless we express it in harmful ways. Ephesians 4:26 says, "When angry, do not sin." Most people do not know how to obey that command.

In all the years that I have worked with people who were angry, I have found only one useful thing about anger: *It gives us energy to use in solving our problems.*

The best example I know of people who have learned to use their anger well is the organization "Mothers Against Drunk Drivers." This organization was started by mothers who lost their children to drunk drivers. I doubt that anyone would blame them if their anger and revenge consumed them for the rest of their lives. If a bereaved mother wanted to shoot anyone who came out of an ABC store and got behind the wheel of a car, we could understand her feelings. Notice that I am not saying that anyone is justified for revenge, but only that we could understand such behavior from someone who has been desperately wounded.

If anger can be so destructive, why did God give us the ability to get angry? How can anger be useful instead of destructive?

Instead, however, many mothers who lost children because of drunk drivers settled on a constructive outlet for their grief. (Note the sections about dealing with anger in chapter 5, "How to Help Someone Who Is Grieving.") They bonded together and used their energies to prevent future deaths of children. They worked to get laws changed. They formed groups for bereaved parents. They attended rehabilitation groups for drunk drivers, expressing their grief in settings that can result in saved lives. Without the energy that comes from their anger, they could not have accomplished such a great, beneficial work.

When we direct the energy that comes with anger in a focused, constructive direction that will honor God, we can escape destruction of ourselves and others.

120

What You Can Do

Perhaps your friend has never thought of herself as an angry person. Or perhaps she knows that she has struggled with anger most of her life. Here are some ways to help.

Begin to define the problem.

If you are trying to help someone determine if anger is a problem, some of the following questions may be useful.

Has someone hurt you?

Are you afraid?

Has this gone on for a long time?

Do you find yourself in the same type of situation over and over?

Do you know what to do when you feel angry?

How do you usually respond?

What effect does your response have? On you? On the one who hurt you?

What is the eventual outcome?

Help your friend face reality.

Help your angry friend see her situation realistically. Encourage her to look honestly at the damage destructive anger has caused in her life. Help her identify specific ways in which she can protect herself by learning to use her anger constructively.

Suggest that when she begins to get angry she pause and ask herself, "How do I really want this to turn out? How does God want this to turn out?" Remind her that she has tremendous influence over the outcome of any situation.

Marla said, "The first thing I had to do was to face my life and marriage honestly, admitting that I was 'living a lie,' which I came to realize was as sinful in God's eyes as anything Clark was doing. I had to forsake my 'sinister' life and accept the risk that I might be the only one who was willing to change, but I decided to obey God and begin to live in truth. More than anything, I wanted to be an authentic person in His Kingdom."

Can you think of others who have directed their anger and frustration into a productive outlet?

Present some alternatives to angry behavior.

If your angry friend has been hurt, read chapter 12 on bitterness and forgiveness. If he or she is fearful and feeling helpless, read chapter 13 on fear. If she is willing, discuss those chapters together.

If there is a long-term frustration, include some problem-solving techniques, helping her find ways to deal with each situation as it arises.

Why do you think it is so difficult to face the truth? What were some of the losses Marla might have experienced due to her decision?

Suggest, for example, that she practice "putting on her pause button" before responding to an intense situation. Encourage her to allow time to pray and think before acting. Help her learn to look for creative alternatives to each situation that tempts her to lose control. Help her practice looking ahead to the potential outcome of each decision.

Encourage her to use her energy in ways that will bring productive changes in her life.

For example, a friend encouraged Marla to go for counseling. As she began to live her life to please God instead of Clark, she was able to admit her anger and forgive Clark, as well as not allow him to mistreat her any longer. She realized that God did not want her to be abused. She became able to love Him in deeper ways and to trust that He would enable her to think and behave differently.

She learned practical ways to protect herself and her children. One day when Clark was verbally assaulting her, she waited until he left the house, packed her bags, took her children and went to a hotel. She let Clark know, in a concrete way, by removing herself and her children from danger, that he could no longer continue to abuse his family. She set the limits that were necessary to bring about change in her home. Marla exchanged her fear for courage and her behavior began to change.

How would you encourage someone who is angry? Could you help her become aware of the clues her body sends when she is getting angry? How could learning to use anger effectively change someone's life?

Most notably, she realized that she was now beginning to treat her children with reasonableness and fairness. This encouraged her to continue.

She resigned from several committees at church and began to take care of herself. She presented her financial needs to Clark and received more money each month. She began to have her hair done and got a massage once a month. She took care of herself in new ways. As she forgave herself, she was able to see herself in a new light. As Marla began to relax and enjoy self-respect, she was able to show her children respect also.

What are some additional ways that someone might need to take care of himself? How could developing self-respect change his life and the lives of those around him?

Here are some questions that you may wish to ask the person you are helping:

Can you identify ways in which your prolonged anger has harmed you or made your situation even worse?

Are you willing to look at the roots of your anger and let God deliver you from "old" anger?

What do you believe God wants you to do? What outcome does He want?

What do you want the outcome to be?

Will you choose God's outcome?

How can you use the energy from your anger constructively? Will you make a list? (Examples: I can use my anger to pray, read God's Word, get information, listen, seek counsel, examine my motives, make wise decisions, follow through with my decisions.) Encourage your friend to make the list as long as possible so that she will see there is no time to be wasted in revenge or stuffing the emotions.

What is the first step you need to take?

The End of Marla's Anger Story

Marla concluded, "I wanted to live a life of truth and love. I wanted God to be in control of my life, instead of my husband. I was tired of being an angry person. I realized that what I do and whom I become is an issue that I must work out with God. It has taken years, but today there is truth and love in my life and marriage, and I wouldn't trade my husband for anyone in the world.

"I pray that I will only become angry at things that Jesus is angry about. I pray that He will continue to help me examine angry feelings and direct them in ways that solve problems and honor Him. Dealing with anger has been a long but profitable journey!"

Scriptures for Meditation

Proverbs 14:29; 15:1; 16:32
Ecclesiastes 7:9
Romans 12:19
Ephesians 4:31–32
James 1:19–20

EIGHT

HOW TO HELP SOMEONE WHO IS DEPRESSED

An attractive young woman named Laura told me of her personal struggles: "Last year my mother died. Two weeks after her death, I discovered that my husband was having an affair. Within the next week, his company transferred us here. I miss my mother . . . my friends . . . my church. My husband and I are trying to renew our marriage, but my heart is broken and I don't trust him. I feel all alone. I can't remember what it was like to feel good. I'm worn out, used up, fed up, disappointed and hopeless! I want to go to bed and sleep my life away! I just don't care anymore."

Have you ever felt as Laura did? Has someone in your family experienced depression?

As you can see from Laura's story, the circumstances that can bring about depression are many and varied. Laura was in the midst of grief following her mother's death. When she needed her husband the most, she dis-

127

covered that he had betrayed her—another grievous blow! When Laura was forced to move, she lost the daily support of her friends and her church. Her recent losses were many.

Laura continued, "Someone told me that I am depressed. I feel so ashamed! Don't I have enough faith? I've always thought Christians should be above depression!"

I have counseled with people for years, and I have consistently observed Christians who believe as Laura did. That kind of shame is based in pride. Depression is not a sin; it is an emotional state. When we think as Laura did, we refuse to face the truth, seek help and receive healing.

Have you thought that believers should be above depression? Do you think depression is a sin? If you do, why?

If you are helping someone who is experiencing depression, read on. It is possible for someone who is depressed to go humbly before the Lord and be lifted up by Him (see 1 Peter 5:6). We will explore ways to understand His great love, His great mercy and His ability to rescue those who are depressed.

Circumstances That Lead to Depression

The circumstances that often precede depression are similar to those that initiate grief. Some of them are:

A death
A job loss
Long periods of extreme stress, anger, grief and
    anxiety
A divorce or betrayal
Rejection

A move
A church change
Health problems
Loss of property or position
Abandonment, neglect or abuse
Guilt, shame and regret

Most of the circumstances listed above had occurred in Laura's life, leaving her depleted emotionally. *The fact that she was a believer did not guarantee that she knew how to cope with long-term, heartbreaking circumstances.* That kind of knowledge comes from training and maturity. Many sincere, faithful believers do not know how to respond to unfair, hurtful circumstances. We can get weighed down and find it almost impossible to get up!

Many people, such as survivors of childhood abuse, have experienced low levels of depression most of their lives. Many abuse survivors do not even realize they are depressed because they have been sad since early childhood. They have not felt good often enough or long enough to make a comparison. They think that life includes a heavy, sad feeling. In fact, any type of childhood trauma can result in depression that simply becomes a way of life. These individuals usually get relief only when a severe crisis later in life drives the depression downward, and they seek help because a variety of symptoms increases and intensifies. Many are surprised to find that they have been depressed! When they receive

> *Have you judged people who have been depressed? Have you thought that they should just "get a grip"? Do you have compassion toward people who become depressed? Would you like to help?*

treatment and begin to feel good for the first time, they are amazed.

Some individuals suffer from a chemical imbalance that causes depression. This type of depression can be more difficult to treat, but treatment is available for most types of depression today. If you are helping someone who is depressed, encourage him to seek help. Challenge him not to be delayed or defeated by false shame and pride.

Do you know people who have been depressed for a long time? If you do, what information do you have about their backgrounds? Do you know people who say they have never been happy?

Symptoms of Depression

In order to help someone who is depressed, you must know the symptoms of depression. They are:

Feelings

Feels sad and hopeless
Is apathetic, bored, has little motivation
Feels guilty
Feels worthless
Feels no one cares
Is easily irritated or angered
Expects the worst

Physical Symptoms

Sleep problems
Significant weight loss or gain

Stomach problems
Chest tightness, shallow breathing
Headaches, chronic aches and pains
Fatigue
Frequent sighing

Behavioral Patterns

May withdraw from people
Loses interest in routine activities
Cannot concentrate
May neglect appearance
Makes pessimistic comments
May discuss suicide or the wish to die
Cries easily
Cannot make decisions
Is restless

Depression is more than just a bad mood. The symptoms I have listed above must be consistent for at least two weeks in order to establish a diagnosis of depression. If these symptoms have persisted for more than two weeks, help is needed.

What about Medication for Depression?

Several years ago, a pastor who had been severely depressed for years came to me for help. He was obviously discouraged. He slumped in his chair and said, "I've been depressed for years! I don't know why God hasn't healed me! I've asked and asked Him to take the depression away and nothing happens!"

I could see that he was disappointed and angry with God. He also appeared to feel that he had failed as a pastor because the depression had continued in spite of his best efforts.

As I listened to him talk I grew more and more certain that medication could help him. Eager to share that information, I responded, "Sir, are you aware that there are excellent medications available today for depression? I feel confident that you can be treated and begin to have a sense of well-being!" I leaned forward in the excitement I felt for him, expecting him to be relieved to hear the good news.

The pastor physically moved away from me, pushing his chair back. His resistance to my suggestion became evident. He replied, "I am a pastor. I have prayed and I believe that God should heal me Himself! I am *not* going to take any of those medications that 'the world' uses! I'll just wait for my prayers to be answered—no matter how long it takes!"

> *Have you been prejudiced against the use of medications? Why? Would you be able to encourage someone to make an appointment with a physician so that he could be evaluated for medication? Do you see any valid reason why it would be wrong to use medication for depression?*

This pastor made a common error. He believed that we can dictate God's methods of healing us just because we have faith! He also rejected methods that God has already provided because they are also available to unbelievers! He felt that being a Christian gave him exalted status and, in his pride, placed himself above others. When he did this, he also placed himself beyond help that was already available.

It is my opinion that this pastor's prayer probably had already been answered. The answer was waiting for him in the pharmacy on the corner. God has blessed us with so many methods of healing from depression. If we will receive, we can begin to recover and regain life.

Note that medication alone is not usually a complete answer for the person suffering from depression. While medication can help with chemical imbalances in the brain, other issues related to the depression usually need to be addressed as well. For example:

Medication cannot change an attitude. We must allow God to change our negativity or impatience.

Medication cannot heal a broken heart. We must grieve, refuse bitterness, and begin to let go and be willing to trust again.

Medication is not a substitute for obedience, and it will not develop stronger character traits.

Medication will not increase knowledge. These issues must be worked out in our day-to-day relationships with God and with the people in our lives.

If medication will not bring about complete deliverance from depression, what is it actually good for? Medication can help someone *feel* like making the changes he needs to make. Anyone who is emotionally depleted does not have the energy to pray, to obey, to make changes in his behavior, to gain the knowledge he needs to have in order to overcome the circumstances that preceded the depression. When someone is depressed, he is often too confused to solve a problem. Medication can clear the mind and lift the mood, increasing energy so that the individual can begin to make the changes he needs to make. By feeling better, he can go about the work of getting better!

If someone you care about is depressed, I suggest that you offer to go with him or her to see a physician. Sometimes when people are depressed, they lack the motivation to move forward. When someone who cares encourages them and accompanies them, it makes all the difference.

A Simple, Effective Plan for Relief from Depression

When hurtful circumstances happen, we feel pain. Often we also feel fear. If the circumstances have been chronic, continuing over a long period of time, we experience frustration. These emotions quickly escalate into anger.

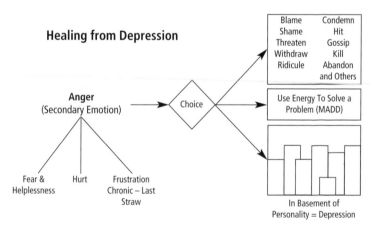

As I stated in chapter 7, some people do not realize that they are angry because anger can be disguised in so many ways. For example, once I worked with a woman from the South. She was depressed, suffering also from muscle tension and gastrointestinal disturbances. She told me, "In my family, ladies are not allowed to be angry. Anger is considered ill-mannered. However, they are allowed to be sad. Therefore, when I am hurt, I let myself cry or withdraw, but never would I express anger! In fact, I don't think I even know what anger feels like!"

We lose sight of our anger because we can disguise it in milder forms. We can simply resent a situation or pout or sulk. We can withdraw and become silent or unavailable. We can deny

Have you ever suggested that a depressed person seek medical treatment? If so, what was his response? What would your response be?

the anger altogether, hiding it from others and ourselves. We can believe that we are sad, but not angry. *Anger becomes a heavy burden, which we internalize. That burden is called depression.*

The heaviness of depression is too much for us to carry. We become hopeless under its weight. Proverbs 12:25 says, "Anxiety in a man's heart weighs it down." Have you heard someone say, "I have a heavy heart"? He is accurately personalizing Scripture!

As you learned in the chapter on anger, anger is unexpressed energy. It precedes action. We can learn to direct our anger in healthy ways. Most often, however, we direct it at others. We blame, accuse, threaten, condemn, ridicule, hit or withdraw and punish through silence. Sometimes when the person retaliates, the pain that comes back toward us is more than we can bear.

If we decide to cease directing our words and actions toward another person, we often push our anger inward, sealing it into the "basements" of our personalities. That is when the energy becomes depression. We have boxes stored in these mental basements that contain our hurts, fears and frustrations. In most cases, the boxes are labeled carefully with the names of the ones who harmed us. The greater the number of boxes stored, the deeper the depression becomes!

Sometimes, when the weight becomes too heavy to carry, in an effort to gain relief, we release the energy from the basement and begin to attack again. We can continue to do that until we feel so bruised that we bury the energy in the basement once more, storing our fresh wounds in new boxes.

Depression creates fatigue because we have to be on guard mentally 24 hours a day in order to keep the door to the basement tightly shut. We know that if the anger is allowed to escape, we will suffer and be defeated once more. Keeping guard on the door is a duty that requires constant attention and energy. As long as we are guarding the door, we do not have the energy left to change our lives.

This is a self-defeating system. If we attack others, they will attack us back. If we retreat and bury our anger, we become weighed down by the heaviness of it.

If we do not attack or bury our anger, what can we do? Is there a more constructive plan? How can you help someone find another place to put his or her anger?

Begin cleaning out the basement.

You can begin by helping your friend see that anger can actually be useful: She can use the energy that comes with anger to make her life better. She can actually profit from it! If your friend does not continue to use her anger to harm, and if she does not store it inside, she can direct her energy into problem solving. Then if someone causes her pain, she can ask God to help her make good choices. The Holy Spirit will help her apply the energy in constructive ways.

When Laura, whose story opened this chapter, decided to stop depositing boxes in the basement of her personality, she reclaimed her own energy. She decided to stop punishing her husband mentally and verbally for being unfaithful to her. She released him and their future together into God's hands. Then she took actions that helped her adjust to her new surroundings. She used some of her energy to find a new church. She joined a Bible study and made new friends. She continued counseling each week and began to clean out her basement. She opened the boxes, made an inventory of the hurts and cleared them out through forgiveness.

Do you have boxes in your basement? How long have they been there? Do you know other people who have stored anger? Do you believe that they are aware of their condition? Do they have heavy hearts? Do they exhibit the symptoms of depression?

If the person you are helping is going to empty the boxes in her basement, she, too, must begin by forgiving those who have harmed her. Forgiveness takes energy.

Laura prayed often for an attitude of grace toward her husband. It took strength for her to discipline herself when she was tempted to remind him of how much he had hurt her. She prayed for wisdom as she agreed to give him a chance to restore trust between them. She began the process of forgiving the woman who had become involved with her husband. It took energy to feel her feelings and release them in prayer.

It was also necessary to forgive herself for ways that she had failed in the marriage. She had to admit those things to herself and ask for God's forgiveness. She faced her anger at God because her mother had not recovered from her illness, as well as anger at her husband's company because it had insisted on relocation at such a difficult time in her life. She went on to face hurts from childhood, high school and college.

> *What are some things you need to do when you have a problem? Can you see that you only have enough energy to take constructive actions? What steps did Laura take that required energy?*

Over several weeks, Laura applied her energy diligently toward emptying the boxes where anger had been stored. The day came when her basement was empty. She had no more stored grievances to carry and no more desire to attack. She was free . . . and her depression had lifted! She was able to move on!

What if the basement is too dark and too full? If you believe that the basement is too deep for the two of you to clean out, offer to go with your friend to a counselor. Then serve as a support person to the counselor with your encouragement and prayer. Be available as needed while your friend opens his boxes, feels his feelings and faces his offenses and hurts with Jesus.

Identify lessons learned.

Remember to help your friend find wisdom. Proverbs 2–4 extols the many virtues of following the path of wisdom. Knowledge will protect your friend in the future and give her a sense of God's protection. Evaluate the process and find times when she made good changes. Then define the rewards that followed. Suggest that she record the wisdom she has gained in a journal.

Never "wait until."

Sometimes people get stuck in depression. Once a woman in a group that I sponsored said that she had been depressed for ten years. As I questioned her about the length of her depression, she said, "My daughter left almost eleven years ago. She hasn't called or written to me since. I will be depressed until she comes home!"

Can you see this woman's decision to remain depressed? She made her choice soon after her daughter left. However, no matter how long she stayed depressed, her decision would not affect her daughter's return. She was making an unnecessary emotional sacrifice. Her depression was not going to magically create the return of her daughter.

If someone appears to be stuck, encourage her not to "wait until" to be joyful. Joy is a fruit of the Holy Spirit. Regardless of life's circumstances, we can always have joy! Joy is available, and there is no good reason to delay it or deprive ourselves of it.

Someone who is depressed need not give up hope. Your gentle and compassionate direction can make a big difference in the choices your friend makes. While the decision to make a change rests with your friend, simply showing her that there are choices and methods she can use is an invaluable service.

Scriptures for Meditation

Psalms 34:17–18; 147:3
Isaiah 40:31; 41:10; 43:2; 51:11; 61:3
Romans 8:38–39
2 Corinthians 1:3–4
Philippians 4:8
1 Peter 4:12–13; 5:6–7

NINE

How to Help Someone Who Has Been Betrayed

There are so many forms of betrayal and rejection that almost no one escapes some contact with them. A husband betrays a wife. A friend tells your secrets. An employer hires you on promise of promotion and then passes you by. You date someone who is dating someone else behind your back. Your business partner takes more than his share of profit. Things are not always as they seem to be.

No matter how it comes, betrayal hurts. It breaks your heart and rips out your ability to trust. It creates doubts about yourself and causes you to become suspicious of innocent people.

During my early twenties, I had a friend named Alicia who was married to a man who verbally assaulted her. John called her fat, crazy and worthless and threatened constantly to leave her. When she found out that he was seeing other women, he finally left, blaming her for his unfaithfulness.

When Alicia told me what had happened, my response was, "I hated the way he treated you. I knew he would probably do this sooner or later. You'll be better off without him. Don't waste your grief."

Have you, or has someone you know, been rejected or betrayed? If so, what was the situation? What was the effect?

Alicia burst into tears and replied, "How could you say that about John? He's my husband! I love him and I'll do anything to get him back!"

As you can see, I failed to give any strength or comfort to Alicia. I had no idea how to help someone who suffered the agonies of betrayal.

What Is Betrayal?

Betrayal happens when someone wants to do something for himself more than he wants to be loyal to you. The root of betrayal is selfishness. Someone chooses an action or a person over you. Betrayal may be a planned, deliberate action, or it may occur when someone gets caught in a snare. Regardless, at some point a decision is made by another person to put his own needs and desires before yours.

For instance, John had been fired from several jobs. He felt angry and humiliated. Justifying his need for consolation, he compensated himself with the company of other women. He did not set out to destroy his marriage, but as time went on he became more and more willing to get his needs met at Alicia's expense. After several months, he fooled himself into thinking that Alicia *deserved* to be forsaken because she could not make the pain of his job losses go away. He decided that he deserved to be compensated. John had problems that he was not willing to face and solve in an honest way. Instead, he made the decision to become an unfaithful husband.

Specific Steps to Take

Someone who has been betrayed will experience many emotions. Here are some ways to help.

Listen carefully; save your opinions.

When I carelessly expressed my opinions about John, I hurt Alicia. The fact that he had betrayed her had not changed her love for him at all. My words offended her. As she turned her anger at John toward me, I realized that I had only added to her distress.

A person who has been betrayed needs time to process. Much of what Alicia had believed about John had suddenly proved false and it was going to take time for her to understand that such a thing could happen. Even though *you* may not be surprised, the person who has been wounded can barely absorb the truth. In fact, Alicia cried, *"How could this have happened? I just can't believe it."*

If you will listen, she may talk her way into the truth. The shock and anger will finally melt away, and she will be ready to face reality. Initially she just is not ready to verbalize what she probably already knows is true.

Expect confusion and self-condemnation.

When Alicia told me that John had left her, she said, "He wouldn't have found someone else if I had given him more support. I should have lost weight! I can learn to meet his needs. I'll lose the weight if he will only come back. It's all my fault."

Often the betrayed person would rather take the blame. This allows more "hopeful" thinking: "I broke it, so I can fix it." If we blame the other person, we have to face the fact that he or she may not ever want to "fix it." Many of us would rather take the blame and feel powerful than blame the other person and feel helpless.

Have you known someone who was not ready to face the truth? How did he continue to deny the truth? What words did he use?

You might want to remind your friend that no one can force another person to betray a loved one. The fact is, the weakness was always there waiting for a good excuse to manifest itself.

At this point, instead of criticizing the one who betrayed or rejected your friend, simply offer affirmation. Point out your friend's good qualities and remind her of the people who love her just as she is. Tell her what she contributes to your life. Be specific. Remind her of past successes. Above all, remind her of who she is in Christ.

Be trustworthy; keep confidences.

Your friend's greatest need is to know that some people can be trusted. When someone has lost the ability to trust, she has truly been robbed because trust is a cornerstone of all relationships.

For example, I worked with a young man named Steve. When his wife, Jennifer, left him, he called the person whom he trusted the most, his small group leader at his church. As he poured out his story, the leader was overcome with sympathy and concern. He also felt inadequate to help, so he asked his wife for advice. Before long, the details of Steve's marriage were public knowledge and his sense of trust was doubly damaged. He began to believe that absolutely no one could be trusted.

Have you ever broken a confidence? Has anyone ever broken yours? What was the result? Do you see breaking confidentiality as betrayal?

When you promise not to tell, *do not tell.* No matter what your motive is, do not tell. Your friend will see your action as deliberate betrayal and she will not turn to you or anyone else any time soon.

Be prepared to go in emotional circles.

One week Alicia wanted John back. The next week, she was glad he was gone. Then she remembered him as the best husband in the world. The next week, he was the worst.

Feelings about herself would vacillate in the same way. She would say, "I just want a chance to be a better wife to John." Then she would say, "You were right. He's always been a jerk! He has probably been unfaithful ever since we got married." Occasionally, she would enlarge her suspicions and say, "You really can't trust men! They're *all* jerks!"

Though your friend may be confused, she will finally come to grips with the truth about herself as well as the one who betrayed her. It is not easy to figure out how someone who loved you could hurt you so badly.

Note: Particularly with broken relationships, caution your friend to be careful about how he or she speaks of the offending person. If down the road attempts are made to reconcile, friends and family will have difficulty supporting a renewed connection with "a jerk." Encourage discernment in unloading thoughts and feelings.

Ask good questions.

Melissa, a woman whose husband left her, told me, "I had a neighbor who asked good questions. She didn't try to tell me what to do, but the questions she asked made me think. After my husband had come and gone a few times, leaving me completely distraught, she asked, 'Why do you want to continue to be married to a man like that?' Her question enabled me to look at my situation more objectively. When I became logical instead of emotional, I asked myself the same question. I could not come up with a good reason to try to get my husband to return home again. For the first time, I began letting him go, and it's a good thing I did because he never came back."

Melissa continued, "Later she asked me, 'What can you do with your life now that you could not do before?' For the first time, I began to see possibilities in my future. Before she asked me that, I felt that my life was over because he had left me."

Good questions will enable your friend to see what she might have missed before and help her develop an optimistic view of her future.

Encourage support from others.

Your friend might benefit greatly from attending a support group. Recently a young person in a support group said, "I felt so much better when I heard other people share their stories. I realized that some very fine people have been abandoned! I went into the meeting feeling like such a hopeless loser, and I left thinking I'm not so bad after all. And I found out that I'm not going crazy, because betrayal makes all of us feel as if we are nuts."

Someone who has been betrayed usually wants to withdraw and become isolated. He feels humiliated and does not want people to know what has happened. Support groups prevent isolation, offer identification and provide a place to process. They can provide a valuable, supportive experience.

Help guard against bitterness.

The time will come when remaining angry will not be beneficial. As we have seen in the last two chapters, it takes a lot of energy to be angry, to rehash the past and to fret about the future. If your friend is going to be able to move ahead with life, he will have to let go of the past and look ahead.

Thomas and his brother began a business together after their graduations from college. For several years, they struggled to become profitable, but finally they began to experience remarkable financial success. At the end of the tenth year of their partnership, Thomas discovered that his brother had embezzled funds from their company. Shocked and enraged, Thomas confronted his brother who admitted that he had been dishonest for the last five years. Thomas agreed not to press charges against him if he resigned from the company. Months went by and Thomas continued to express anger toward his brother.

Are you familiar with various resources in your area? What types of support groups are available? Can you see why someone would be embarrassed because of what another person has done?

One day he was surprised to find himself considering various ways in which he could avoid paying his taxes. For the first time, Thomas was becoming dishonest, too. How did this happen?

When we have been betrayed, we can find many ways to compensate ourselves. Thomas thought, *I can find ways to make up the money I lost.* His unresolved anger led him to consider doing exactly what his brother had done. How did that happen? *We become like the people we think about all the time.* When Thomas allowed angry thoughts of his brother to dominate his mind, he gradually began to think about doing the same thing his brother had done! (Read chapter 12 on bitterness.)

Unforgiveness binds us to the one who has betrayed us. Forgiveness cuts the tie to the past, enabling us to move on and to become like Jesus.

Encourage your friend to forgive. Inform him that it is the most self-protective action he can take. The one who betrayed him may not benefit, but your friend surely will.

Is Restoration Possible?

Yes, restoration is possible, but not everyone who has been guilty of betrayal is willing to do the work of rebuilding trust with the person he or she harmed. Others resist repentance. They simply do not have the humility to go through the process that may be required.

Your friend will need to define, with God's help, what it will take for trust to be built again. He will need to consider his requirements carefully because he will be placing his heart on the line again.

I worked with a couple, Steve and Carol, who had separated because she had had an affair. If Carol was five minutes late getting home from work, Steve would be suspicious. Carol said, "I *told* him that I would be faithful! What do I have to do to prove that?" If she wanted to gain her husband's trust, Carol would have to do more than arrive at home on time. A wounded heart does not recover quickly. When requirements are made, they must add up to an expression of firm commitment.

Have you ever had to earn someone's trust after you had broken it? How did you feel? Has anyone ever needed to earn your trust? Were they willing to do what was required?

Ask your friend what proof he will need, and ask him to define exactly what must be done. Suggest that he communicate his needs before reconciliation is attempted.

Steve asked Carol to call him when she left her office, letting him know that she would be late. Carol agreed to do so because, even though she hated to have to report in, she also wanted her marriage restored. She realized that there was a price to pay for the betrayal, and she was willing to pay it.

Learning from Jesus

Jesus was betrayed by Judas and by Peter (see John 13:21–30; Matthew 26:69–75). When Judas faced his sin, he killed himself. When Peter faced his sin, he humbled himself. At Pentecost, Peter received the power of the Holy Spirit and preached a mighty sermon, by which three thousand people were saved (see Acts 2:41). From that time on, Peter was faithful. Tradition states that he died at the hands of godless men by being hung upside down on a cross. He abandoned himself to serving God and learned to be faithful to the end.

Jesus shows us that if the one who betrayed repents and proves to be faithful, he or she does not need to be punished any longer.

Can you compare the responses of Judas to those of Peter? Why do you believe Judas chose to kill himself? Why do you think Peter chose to repent and follow Jesus?

After Jesus' death and burial, three women went to His tomb to anoint His body with spices. They found the stone rolled away from the tomb, and going inside they were amazed to see a young man in a white robe. He said,

> Do not be amazed and terrified; you are looking for Jesus of Nazareth Who was crucified. He is risen; He is not here. See the place where they laid Him. But be going; tell the disciples and Peter, He goes before you into Galilee; you will see Him there, [just] as He told you.
>
> Mark 16:6–7

Peter's name was the only one mentioned specifically. Why was this? I believe that Jesus wanted Peter to know that He still wanted his friendship.

If you have been hurt, have you been tempted to let your distrust "spread"? If you have, how has it affected your life? Have you "missed" love that was available to you?

When someone who has been hurt genuinely wants a relationship restored, he needs to be open to see how God will work. It takes great courage to open his heart again to someone who has betrayed him, but if he does not, he may find himself closing his heart to those who have not hurt him at all.

Is there a blessing for someone who has been betrayed? Yes. *The blessing that comes from distrust of people is more trust in Jesus.* Most of us tend to rely on human beings as long as we can. The sooner we realize that Jesus is the only Person whom we can really trust to care, to be faithful, to meet our needs and to love us totally, the better our lives will be. We will be able to see people as *they* really are and Jesus as *He* really is, and we will begin to put our hearts in order again.

Scriptures for Meditation

Deuteronomy 31:6
Psalms 4:8; 46:1; 91:1–2; 147:3
Isaiah 26:3
John 14:1, 18, 27

TEN

HOW TO HELP SOMEONE WITH A POOR SELF-IMAGE

Last year I spoke at a retreat for single women. I arrived early so that I would have time to mingle with some of the women in the lobby before the first session began. A pretty young woman named Sandy came up to me and whispered, "I'm so glad you are going to speak on self-esteem! I am thirty years old and I thought some man would have chosen me by now. All my friends are married, and I've been a bridesmaid more times than I can count."

At that moment we were given the signal to enter the conference room. As women surged past us, she grabbed my arm and continued, "I know I'm not really pretty. I'm not very smart. I don't earn enough to buy the clothes I need to attract a man. Not only that, I'm about ten pounds overweight. I'm so disappointed in myself! I hope you can help me. I really want to get married. How can I get a man to choose me?"

153

Sandy was mixed-up about *who she is* as opposed to *getting what she wants!* Many factors determine what happens in our lives. *Who we are* is not the only factor. When we cannot *get what we want,* we decide that *who we are* is not good enough and condemn ourselves for it.

Do you believe that many people are working hard to become lovable? Do you think the system works? If not, why?

Hundreds of articles, books and seminars in the last twenty years have guided us in the search for high self-esteem. And most of us have undertaken this search for one reason: We believe that we can become good enough to be lovable.

Many believe that we will be loved *if* we are handsome or beautiful, *if* we behave right, dress well, go to the right schools, accomplish enough, come from the right families, get enough education, make enough money . . . and are *thin!* We spend hours trying to fix ourselves. When we cannot make our self-esteem system work, we give up on ourselves.

The Real Need

In a world filled with makeovers and cover-ups, how can we know who or what is real? Recently I read a magazine article that illustrated a beautiful woman with a perfect figure. I was surprised to discover that only her eyes and eyebrows were really her own. Her photograph had been computer adjusted! She had someone else's nose, chin and hair. She weighed about forty pounds more than the woman in the photo. The real person was lost in an effort to present the *perfect* woman.

Many of us have allowed ourselves to be "adjusted" to create an image. Our lives reflect the confusion and brokenness that come when we allow ourselves to sacrifice our true identities.

At a party last week, I was introduced to Joseph, the thirty-year-old son of a friend of mine. As we approached the buffet table, I said, "Joseph, tell me about yourself." Although he seemed outgoing and intelligent, Joseph gave me a blank look, shrugged and replied, "Well, I guess there's not much to tell."

Many of us would respond similarly. We do not know ourselves very well. We reject what we do know. We have not found our purposes in life. Our dreams have been sabotaged. We have let others define whom we have become. We do not feel loved. That is where the problem lies.

How Love Works

Years ago my husband, Wayne, and I used to visit both sets of parents on Sunday afternoons. Between the two towns where they lived was a large state prison. When we drove within a mile of the prison we had to stop because of the crowds. Sunday was visitors' day. Cars were pulled to the sides of the road, and groups of women and children walked toward the prison gate. Usually they carried picnic baskets and colorfully wrapped gifts. They smiled and chatted with one another as they eagerly moved along.

As we neared the gate we could see prisoners gripping the tall chain link fence that surrounded the prison. As I looked at the dark, brooding expressions on most of the faces, I thought invariably, *These men are criminals. They have obviously been convicted of terrible crimes. They may have battered and abused these very*

155

women and children! How do they get their families to come here Sunday after Sunday, bringing gifts?

On one of our trips, the Lord spoke to me: There is nothing that these men can do to make their families continue to come. They come because they have love in their hearts. *Nothing the men could do or say* could cause this to happen.

At that point, I learned some valuable lessons.

> *If love is not in someone's heart, he cannot love me.*
> *If he has love and chooses to withhold it, there is nothing I can do.*
> *If someone is able to love and chooses to love me, he will.*
> *Whether or not I am loved is up to the other person.*

Through the years, when I have seen people strive so hard to earn love or to prove that they are lovable, I tell them the story of the prison. We will never be good enough to *earn* love. Even if we can get people to admire us, they may not love us. They may actually envy us, but their envy will only promote competition, not love.

Jesus showed us how love really works. Romans 5:8 tells us that while we were still sinners, Jesus came to earth and died for us. By the time most of us come to Jesus, we are broken, guilty, ashamed, confused, discouraged, angry, wounded. We are somewhat like the prisoners. We are not a pretty sight. We have not proven to be very smart or successful in life . . . *or thin.*

Would you rather be admired or loved? Envied or loved? Why?

Jesus embraces us just as we are, and that is what love truly is. Jesus loves us when our self-image is at the lowest point. Loving is up to Him because when we come to Him, most of us bring nothing. That is how true love really works.

Who Are You, Really?

Many of us exist within the framework of words that have been spoken to or about us. Proverbs 18:21 says that life and death are in the power of the tongue. Words can have an impact that lasts for years. In fact, they have the power to shape a life.

For example, I asked this question in one of my small groups: "Can you recall words that have affected whom you have become and what you do? And how long ago were those words spoken?"

Immediately a hand went up. A man named George replied, "I remember words that were spoken thirty-five years ago. When I was ten years old, my father announced proudly at a Thanksgiving dinner that I was going to be a doctor when I grew up. My father was a renowned surgeon, and it was his desire that I follow in his footsteps. As I grew older, I exhibited talent as an artist. I received a lot of recognition for my painting. My favorite teacher encouraged me to study art at the university and apply for scholarships abroad."

George leaned forward, tears coming into his eyes, "Each time I painted, I felt such joy! Then I would remind myself, *I can't be an artist because I'm supposed to be a doctor.*"

In an effort to please his father and use his own gifts, George became a plastic surgeon—a combination of sorts of doctor and painter! He continued, "The words that my father spoke determined the course of my life. When I was a child, I didn't know that his word wasn't the law. I have continued to live as if I have no choice.

Now I see that I have a God-given right to choose His plan for me."

For years George lived the life he felt obligated to live to please his father. Then, in mid-life, he could no longer bear the burden of his decision. He gave up a thriving medical practice to become a full-time artist. The power of his father's words no longer controlled who he was and what he became.

When George told his father of his decision, he received quite a surprise: His father actually supported his decision to become an artist. George's father had meant to give his son a compliment all those years ago, not a mandate! George had been living under a false burden created by words.

> *Can you recall words that were spoken to you that had a powerful effect upon your life? Were they positive or negative? How did they affect your future decisions?*

If your friend has a poor self-image because he has allowed someone to take over his life, be advised: Those who take over other people's lives seldom give them back. They keep and use them for their own purposes for as long as they are allowed to do so. If your friend has been molded into a false design, encourage him to begin searching for his authentic self—the one that God created.

Has your friend forgotten who he or she really is? God has the answer. He has always known who we are! Look at the words He spoke to the prophet Jeremiah: "Before I formed you in the womb I knew and approved of you [as My chosen instrument], and before you were born I separated and set you apart, consecrating you" (Jeremiah 1:5).

King David pondered this amazing truth as well: "Your eyes saw my unformed substance, and in Your book all the days of my life were written, before ever they took shape, when as yet there was none of them" (Psalm 139:16).

Recent DNA studies tell us that everything about a person is encoded. Our DNA can tell how large our feet will grow, the color of our hair and skin, and how tall we will be. The size of each brain has been predetermined. Our gifts and talents are already programmed. Even our fingerprints are originals! We have been thoughtfully and deliberately created.

God chose to create us. He designed us, called us and produced us. He is the only one who can tell us who we are and why we are here.

The only way that your friend can know who he truly is—the perfect plan that God has in mind for his life—is to ask Him, but he must know Him to ask Him.

How Can Your Friend Know God?

Many people believe that Jesus is God, but they may simply believe a historical account. He has not become real to them, so when they ask Him a question they do not hear His answer. It is similar to reading a book about George Washington, believing that he was the father of our country and first President of the United States, and then looking at his portrait and asking it a question. No matter what you may know about him, this is not a real interaction.

Acts 16:31 gives us the meaning of the work *believe:* "Believe in and on the Lord Jesus Christ—that is, give yourself up to Him, take yourself out of your own keeping and entrust yourself into His keeping, and you will be saved." *Belief is a personal action of surrender, not just an agreement with historical facts.*

159

If we are going to know Him, we must give ourselves to Him in absolute surrender. When we do this, God sends the Holy Spirit to live inside us, establishing a whole new dimension. Then we can begin to know Him and ask Him questions to find guidance for our lives.

When we give Jesus our lives, an inner, spiritual transaction takes place (see 2 Corinthians 5:17). We have an inner connection with God that was not there before (see Colossians 1:13–14). We can hear His voice (see John 10:4). We can walk with Him day by day. Jesus becomes *real*. We begin to sense Him moving in and around us, directing our lives as we follow Him (see Philippians 2:13). Our potential is unleashed and we can begin to become who we were designed to be!

Release from People-Pleasing

Once your friend begins to understand more fully that God has created him as wholly unique, he will begin to see the importance of looking to God for approval as opposed to relying on what others think he should be or do.

Granted, most of us struggle at times with pleasing people. When we are children, we learn to obey our parents. As we grow up, we need to assume more and more responsibility for our own desires and decisions. Many of us simply shift our obedience from our parents to other people. The truth is, we only have to obey those who have legitimate authority over us.

For example, my parents were forty years old when I was born. My mother was a fragile person, and I grew up with a strong awareness that whatever I did affected her moods significantly. I learned at an early age how to keep her happy. I thought that was my job in life.

As I grew older, I transferred this mindset to my friends. Anytime they grew displeased with me, I felt as if I had done something *wrong.* It never occurred to me that *they* might be wrong in their expectations, requests or demands of me.

Observing my conflicts, a wise spiritual mentor once asked me a key question: *Would you rather be loved or used?*

Love and approval are not the same thing. Love is what we need. We can enjoy approval and admiration, but maintaining them requires hyper-vigilance and constant effort. Even then we seldom measure up.

"But don't we need love from people?" you may ask. "Aren't there times when we need their approval?"

We do need love from people. And there are times when we need approval. Luke 2:52 tells us that Jesus had the love and approval of God as well as man: "And Jesus increased in wisdom (in broad and full understanding), and in stature and years and in favor with God and man." Notice the distinction, though: Jesus did not try to earn favor from people. God *gave* Him favor. When we need favor with people, God will grant it according to His purposes.

Are there people whom you work to please? If so, are they high-maintenance people? Are you able to maintain your own emotional stability in such a relationship? Do you believe that you are living authentically?

For example, Queen Esther needed acceptance and approval from King Ahasuerus. Because of the favor she was given, an entire nation was saved and God's purposes were accomplished.

Here are some ways to help your friend gain a good self-image.

Get a jumpstart to a good self-image.

A clear conscience is the fastest way to a good self-image. If the person you are helping feels guilty or ashamed about who she is or what she has done, she is likely full of self-condemnation. How can she allow others to love her if she condemns herself?

Here are a few questions you might want to ask your friend:

Is there anything that you hold against yourself?

Do you need a clear conscience?

Would you let yourself receive love or joy if you didn't feel guilty?

Do you believe that God will forgive you?

Will you let Jesus take your guilt and shame away?

What would it take for you to "get on your own team"?

For further reference, my book *An Invitation to Healing* includes a section that explains the various ways that we sabotage our lives or make ourselves sick by holding our past sins and mistakes against ourselves. Guilt and shame prevent us from experiencing love.

Become your own friend.

A friend of mine was an excellent tennis player during her twenties and thirties. As she got a little older, she began to have problems with her knees. One day we met for lunch and she said, "I'm not ever going to play tennis again! It's just no fun anymore."

When I asked her what had changed, she said, "Well, I miss too many balls. Today I swung at a ball and missed it because I couldn't get there fast enough. I finally ran back to pick up the ball saying to myself, *You're so stupid! Anybody could have hit that one!*"

I responded, "Well, no wonder you don't like to play tennis anymore. You beat yourself up all the time. Can you give yourself some compassion and forgiveness?"

Are you hard on yourself? If you are, do you find self-punishment helpful? Does it encourage you?

She asked, "How could I do that?"

"Well, when you miss another ball, why not stop punishing yourself and be kind to yourself instead? Say something like, 'That's okay, Sweet Thing! You'll get the next one'?"

She sat there dumbfounded. Then she agreed to treat herself kindly the next time.

If we are going to be a friend to ourselves, we must decide to accept the fact that we are not perfect and will never, ever be perfect. We can, however, know that we are being perfected (2 Corinthians 3:18) and that is all that is asked.

Seek God's redemption.

Encourage your friend with the fact that no matter what we have done, we can still recapture God's original design for us. No matter how twisted and broken we may be, we can still be restored to His calling and purposes for our lives.

Larry was a young pastor who had an affair with his secretary. Although he was in his early thirties, he had successfully pastored a large, growing church. After his affair was discovered, he felt as if his life were over.

"No church will ever let me pastor again," he said. "God's anointing is no longer over me. My calling as a pastor is gone. I will never be allowed to minister as God's man again."

Romans 11:29 offered great hope to Larry as he read, "For God's gifts and His call are irrevocable—He never withdraws them when once they are given, and He does not change His mind about those to whom He gives His grace or to whom He sends His call."

Have you ever felt that you had no more chances? Did that turn out to be true? Do you know someone who sinned or made mistakes and then became better than ever?

Larry believed that no church would ever allow him to pastor again. However, God's Word still stands. In fact, his gifts were defined as he drew closer to God. As he went through a year of counseling, restoration and restitution, his humility and his dedication to personal change were so remarkable that he was sought by another church to direct its new recovery program.

No matter what we have done, God's design for us can be redeemed and His purposes for our lives can be fulfilled.

Believe that you have a purpose.

Ephesians 2:10 tells us that God chose us before the foundation of the world, and He has made a plan for each person's life. That plan did not magically come into being when we reached a certain age, graduated from school or opened a business. It is not just a good idea or a "suggestion from heaven." Each of us has a carefully constructed plan that suits us perfectly. We must let Him lead us to it. When we find it, there will be joy and fulfillment. There is a place for everyone!

For example, before Jeremiah was born, God called him to be a prophet to the nations (see Jeremiah 1:4–5). Before Samson was born, God told his mother that Samson would be one of the first people to begin delivering the Israelites from the Philistines (see Judges 13:2–5). Before John was born, God announced his birth to his mother, Elizabeth. Later his father, Zachariah, prophesied that John would be a forerunner to the Messiah (see Luke 1:11–13).

There is a plan for every person. If we do not seek to live as the persons we were created to be, we will not thrive in this life.

Study God's love.

Since the real need is not for self-esteem but for love, suggest that your friend study Scriptures about God's love. It is impossible to look at the life of Jesus, the cross, the work of the Holy Spirit and eternity without becoming convinced of His love.

Suggest for starters that your friend read Ephesians and Colossians. Note the phrases that begin with *In Him*. Ask your friend to write a personal introduction of himself or herself according to Scripture.

Here is mine, for example: "I am Lynda Elliott. I have been redeemed, so I am clean. I have been delivered from the power of the evil one. I have God's favor. I have been chosen, appointed and designed for His purposes. I have heard the truth, and I am stamped with the seal of the Holy Spirit. I have wisdom and I can receive revelation. I have been flooded with Light. I have been set apart, and I know the surpassing greatness of God's power."

We already have an identity that cannot be surpassed. We did not create it, produce it or earn it. It has been prepared and given to us by God. If people can love us, they will. If they cannot or will not, God will always love us. If we need favor, God will grant it. We are free to be exactly who we really are!

Now forget about yourself.

We do not have to carry the burden of who we are, what we become or what we do in life. We can afford to forget about ourselves. God will always remember who we are and what we need. In Mark 8:34 Jesus says, "If anyone intends to come after Me, let him deny himself—forget, ignore, disown, lose sight of himself and his own interests—and take up his cross, and . . . follow with Me."

What is the cross that each of us must carry?

Our crosses are not the trials that come to everyone in life. Our crosses are the difficulties and possible persecution that we may encounter for His sake.

> *How would you introduce your-self scripturally? Do you believe that there is a purpose for your life that you have not discovered yet?*

Rewards will follow. Our good works are recorded in heaven. In Matthew 10:42 Jesus says, "And whoever gives to one of these little ones [in rank or influence] even a cup of cold water because he is My disciple, surely, I declare to you, he shall not lose his reward."

You and I pick up our crosses every time we choose to act in His name. We will be recompensed for what we do. When we understand who we really are and begin to experience His care for us, we can easily begin to forget about ourselves.

In time your friend will learn the truth about who he or she is in Christ. It is a stunning discovery and the beginning of a process in which a poor self-image recedes and love truly has a chance to grow.

Scriptures for Meditation

Psalm 139
Matthew 5:11; 13:23

About Rewards:

Matthew 10:42
Luke 6:35
Hebrews 11:6
2 John 8
Revelation 22:12

 ELEVEN

How to Help Women and Children Who Are Being Abused

Years ago I worked as Recovery Director at a shelter for battered, homeless women and children. Compassionate citizens of Little Rock had provided a safe place for them, a lovely two-story dwelling called Dorcas House.

When a woman entered Dorcas House, she found herself standing in a beautiful foyer with a sparkling chandelier that hung from the second floor. Standing on a mauve carpet, she faced a staircase where someone had placed fresh flowers on a nearby credenza. After she signed in, she was taken to a bedroom on the second floor. She and her children were invited to make themselves comfortable in a room with matching bedspreads and cheerful curtains.

A generous contributor had provided a chapel that contained an organ, a piano and a stained-glass window. A quiet, safe place of worship was available at any time day or night.

Although every effort was made to create an atmosphere of safety, acceptance and hope, the effects of abuse were still devastating. Much prayer, support, education and practical help are needed to help someone who is abused to leave a harmful environment and find a new way of living. The women arriving at Dorcas House were able to take a first step into a life that was free from fear and abuse.

According to Brenda Branson and Paula Silva of Focus Ministries, a not-for-profit organization that educates and provides spiritual and emotional support for women who are being abused, up to six million women are believed to be beaten in their homes each year. In fact, on the average, *a woman is battered in the United States by a partner every nine seconds.* Thousands of women and children are in danger. Sooner or later, most of us will encounter some of them because battered women come from all racial, socioeconomic and educational groups.

Have you ever visited or stayed in a shelter? If so, how did you feel upon arrival? If not, how do you think a woman would feel? What would she need most?

Sadly, there are in the world today many types of abuse and abusers. We will discuss in this chapter the specific needs of battered women and children. If you suspect that the person you are helping suffers from any other form of abuse, such as elder-abuse or the physical abuse of men by women, call the appropriate authorities in your area to get information on ways that you can help.

Identifying Abuse

When I worked at Dorcas House, people in the community asked some interesting questions. If you have never been abused, perhaps these are the same questions you may have.

What are the signs of abuse?

Suspect abuse if a woman or child:

1. has visible injuries such as bruises or cuts that are not consistent with their explanations ("I just fell down the stairs" or "I bump into everything")
2. wears long sleeves or slacks out of season
3. is reluctant to invite others to her home
4. appears fearful, edgy, withdrawn or often has mood swings
5. experiences depression, shame or appears to feel guilty, has a low self-image
6. does not show up at meetings, changes plans at the last minute
7. is guarded, secretive or overly protective of her husband and excuses or justifies his behavior to others; blames herself
8. tries to cover marks with heavy makeup

Why do women stay with men who beat them? Why do they go back?

According to Focus Ministries, here are some reasons why women allow themselves to stay in a dangerous environment.

They believe the mixed messages they are given by those who abuse them. Men who batter women are moody

171

individuals who may worship a woman one day and condemn her the next. These extremes, which make no sense to a woman, keep her off-balance, doubting herself and her own ability to make good decisions.

For example, a dear young woman named Sarah told me that her husband beat her one night and called her a fool and a coward when she locked herself in the bathroom for safety. The next night, he brought flowers and took her to a nice restaurant where he told her what a wonderful wife she was and how he planned to take her on a cruise.

> *As you look over the list, can you recall women who have exhibited several of those symptoms? If so, which ones? Why do you think a woman would hide her bruises?*

They believe that they are at fault. Most batterers blame their victims for the abuse. They make statements such as, "If you would just have supper ready, I wouldn't have to hit you!" or "If you do what I say, you won't get hurt. You made me hit you. It's your own fault!"

Many women are ashamed because they have not been able to make the break from the abuser. They are ashamed to admit their helplessness, to show their bruises or to admit that they have allowed themselves to be abused continually.

Batterers blackmail and intimidate their victims. They may say: "Nobody will believe you. I'm a community leader. I have an excellent reputation. You'll just look like a fool if you tell." Or "If you try to leave, I'll get custody of these kids and you'll never see them again." Contrary to public opinion, many batterers do appear to be outstanding members of their communities, and many people would find it hard to believe the cruelty they inflict on their wives and children.

172

For example, a prominent physician was well known for his warm, kindly bedside manner. At home he was a tyrant. When his wife failed to keep the house as he thought it should be, he took away her checkbook. He barely gave her enough money to buy groceries. In order to have some money to be able to have lunch with her friends, she would buy two large boxes of laundry detergent and then return one of the boxes for a cash refund. She worked part-time in an antique shop, but he demanded that she turn her small check over to him each month because "she wasn't capable of handling money."

They pity the abuser. Because many batterers were abused as children, or have substance-abuse problems, their wives tend to feel sorry for them. In the beginning of their relationship, the women believed that they could "help" their abusers. They find it hard to admit defeat.

Even though many batterers do come from abusive backgrounds, allowing them to abuse others is not going to help them. It will only enable them to perpetuate the cycle that began in childhood. Many will only cease to abuse when they have no target for their anger.

> *Can you understand why a woman might be hesitant to leave a man who batters her? Can you see why she might minimize the harm? Which of her reasons can you most easily understand?*

They minimize the pain. They will say, "It doesn't really hurt so bad" and "He didn't really mean what he said. He was just mad about work." As long as a woman believes that the abuser is just "temporarily out of control," she does not have to take the abuse personally. If she does not believe that she can take care of herself and her children, believing the lie will enable her to continue trying to make her unsafe environment "safe" without having to venture out on her own.

Last year a woman who was in tears exclaimed, "I feel like a prostitute! I don't have the confidence to leave home. I don't have a profession or any kind of job training. I don't think I could earn much. Now, my children and I have everything we need. I know I'm just staying with my husband because he is a good provider of material things. I know that I'm just letting myself be bought, because when I just can't stand it anymore I go on a trip. When I come home, he's usually very nice to me for a few weeks. Overall, life could be a lot worse."

They have false hope. Many battered women say, "Things will change" or "I know he'll get help eventually" or "My love will change him. He'll see and he'll change."

Exactly what behaviors qualify as abuse?

There are three categories of abuse:

Physical abuse: slapping, choking, hitting, restraining, throwing objects, twisting limbs, as well as other forms of violence that may or may not leave marks or bruises

Emotional abuse: ridiculing, name-calling, threatening, shaming, withholding funds or other necessities, accusing, condemning, and embarrassing and shaming the victim publicly

Sexual abuse: rape, forcing sexual behaviors that are feared or not desired

174

How Can I Help a Woman Who Is Being Abused?

Brenda Branson, president of Focus Ministries, offers this excellent list of things you can do.

The most important thing you can do is to believe her. A person who has been abused trusts almost no one. She sees herself as worthless and unlovable. Because she will not expect you to care, she will not think that confiding in you could possibly result in assistance. If someone who is being abused finally gets the courage to tell you, *believe her.* When she sees that you believe her, she will experience her first ray of hope.

Do not assume that someone who is abused knows that you believe her. Verbalize your belief. Reassure her with words like "I am so sorry this is happening." Or "Nobody deserves to be treated like this. In fact, it's against the law."

Identify with her emotions. You might say, "It hurts me to see that you have suffered like this" or "It makes me angry to see what is happening to you!" Let her see that your response is genuine and deep.

Get informed. Order the information packet from Focus Ministries. (Ordering information is provided at the end of this chapter.) Read it and share it with your hurting friend. Use it to inform others of the devastation of abuse.

Take photos of bruises so that the abuse will be clearly documented. Suggest that she make a daily diary, describing various types of abuse. This will also help her confirm the fact that she is being abused. Women who have been abused often begin to doubt that the abuse is really happening. They can

175

become numb to their own feelings and seldom allow themselves to believe the pain. When they record the facts in black and white, it will not be so easy for them to avoid the truth.

Investigate the resources in your area. Locate telephone numbers of shelters and offer to go with her to visit them. Write down the directions to the shelters and encourage her to keep them available in case she needs to make an emergency exit from her home.

Suggest that she get an extra set of car keys made. Suggest that she keep them outside her house in a concealed location.

Encourage her to keep a bag packed with whatever items she might need in order to live for a few days, including special toys for her children. She may need to hide her bag in the trunk of her car, or leave it with you or a relative.

Suggest that she save some cash. If she is unable to do so, give a gift of money. If she needs a significant amount, ask if she would be willing to receive that money as a gift. Funds may be necessary for plane fare, down-payment on an apartment, gas for the car. If she is willing to receive, ask your church to make a donation. Keep the name of the one you are helping confidential. Be sure that she has change available for a pay phone. Or you may want to provide a cell phone.

Ask if she will make two lists. One is a list of all the reasons to leave the dangerous home. The other is a list of everything that might be needed later on, such as medical records, the deed to her house, the title to her car and insurance information.

Be sure that she has the National Domestic Violence Hotline number: 1-800-799-7233.

When you have taken these steps with a woman who is being abused, she will no longer be forced to live in danger. Knowing that someone believes in her and cares enough to help her find a way of escape will go a long way toward taking steps to safety.

What Is Child Abuse?

According to law, child abuse is described as any mistreatment of a child, other than by accidental means, that is perpetrated by an adult.

What are the indicators of child abuse?

There are three categories of child abuse.

Physical Abuse: includes hitting, shaking, burning with cigarettes, hot water or placing a child on a heater, and locking a child in a confined space. Injuries from child abuse include: skull fractures, brain, eye and ear damage, broken bones, severe burns, lacerations and damage to inner organs.

The first abused child I ever saw was a four-year-old little boy who was bleeding from his kidneys. There were deep purple bruises on his buttocks where he had been repeatedly hit with a paddle.

I have seen children who looked like they had impetigo, but their scabs were actually covering wounds from cigarette burns. I have seen babies who were afraid to take a bottle because their mother had crammed the bottle into their mouth because they were eating too slowly, and I have seen children whose feet were scalded after their mother deliberately placed them in a hot bath. One father threw his three-year-old into the wall, causing a skull fracture.

177

Abused children are helpless to protect themselves. They are not allowed to express anger or to resist mistreatment. They cannot escape from their abusers. Their lives are being formed in distorted ways, day by day and night by night. They are usually silent sufferers who live in fear of those who should be protecting them from harm.

Can you recall cruel words that were spoken to you? If so, how did you feel? What effect did they have on you? Do you know someone who is a survivor of emotional abuse? What is he or she like?

Emotional abuse: includes harsh threatening, ridiculing, belittling, frightening, teasing, humiliating, condemning and blaming the child for the family problems. Proverbs 18:21 says that life and death are in the power of the tongue. I have seen the truth of that statement.

Did you think that sexual abuse was qualified by intercourse? Can you see how the other forms of sexual abuse could be just as harmful?

For several years, I sponsored a Parents Anonymous group. Some of the damaging words members of the group recalled were:

"If I hadn't had you, my life would have been different!"

"You look like your father, and he was a no-good loser."

"I ought to send you away and never let you come back!"

"I ought to slap you across this room!"

178

"I wish you had never been born!"

"My life would be a lot easier without you!"

"You're the troublemaker in this family."

"If you would behave, I wouldn't have to treat you this way."

Many of the group members had served time in prison because of abuse to their spouses or children. Others had committed other types of violent crimes. The anger that they were forced to conceal as children surfaced and exploded in adulthood, causing them to continue the cycle of assault.

Sexual abuse: includes not only sexual intercourse, but also fondling a child's genitals, attempted rape, oral sex or exposing by the offender, requiring a child to touch his genitals or sexually explicit speech or any type of sexual exploitation through pornography or prostitution.

Years ago a woman said, "My father never actually had sex with me. There was no intercourse. However, there are several ways to 'have sex' which are harmful to a child."

She continued, "He never caused me any kind of pain, but he fondled me every night and made me touch him. I never knew his behavior could be categorized as abuse."

Although her father did not cause physical pain, he conditioned her gradually until she became an innocent participant in the sexual abuse. The severe emotional pain that followed the years of his sexual abuse showed evidence of the harm he had done.

179

What Can I Do to Protect Children from Abuse?

Know the signs and symptoms of abuse.

Although the symptoms may not necessarily indicate that a child is being abused, they indicate the possibility of abuse and should be investigated.

Some signs that a child is being sexually abused are:

Being overly affectionate in a sexual way inappropriate to a child's age

Medical problems, such as chronic itching, pain in the genitals

Personality changes, such as becoming withdrawn or insecure and clinging

Sudden loss of appetite or compulsive eating

Inability to concentrate, poor grades

Lack of trust or fear of someone they know well

Starting to wet the bed

Nightmares

Becoming anxious about clothing being removed

Drawing sexually explicit pictures

Some signs that a child is being emotionally abused are:

Physical, mental and emotional development lags

Sudden speech disorders

Self-depreciation ("I am stupid, ugly")

Overreacting to mistakes, becoming perfectionistic

Chronic anxiety about new situations

Hair-twisting, rocking, nail-biting or other repetitive behaviors

Some signs that a child is being physically abused are:

Unexplained recurrent injuries or burns
Improbable explanations for marks
Wearing clothes to cover injuries, even in hot weather
Refusing to undress for gym
Fears about medical exams
Fear of personal touch, shrinking back
Fear of contact with abuser

If you suspect that a child is being abused, call the Child Abuse Hotline at 1-800-422-4453.

If you are reluctant to call, remember that it is not your job to confirm the abuse. You must only suspect abuse for your call to be considered legitimate. Professionals at the hotline will report the suspected abuse to proper authorities in your area. Trained personnel will be sent to the home to determine whether or not a child is actually being abused. Your part is simply to make the call, explaining why you suspect abuse. If possible, be prepared to provide the names of the parents and their address and the day care, kindergarten or school the child attends.

Do you have any resistance to reporting abuse? If you do, what is it? What do you think is the right thing to do? How would you feel if you failed to report suspected abuse and a child was later seriously injured?

In fact, all private citizens are required to report suspected child abuse. Schools, psychologists, social workers, professional counselors, physicians, medical personnel and teachers can be held liable for prosecution if they suspect abuse and fail to report it.

181

Your report will be kept confidential, so there is never a reason to fail a child by not reporting suspected abuse.

Our Father takes harm to children very seriously. Those who do not prevent harm are equally responsible. In Matthew 18:10, Jesus says, "Beware that you do not despise or feel scornful toward or think little of one of these little ones, for I tell you that in heaven their angels always are in the presence of and look upon the face of My Father Who is in Heaven."

As observers, we must respect His words and neither abuse nor fail to protect the children that God has sent into this world.

For further information contact: **Focus Ministries, P.O. Box 323, Hanson, KY 42413; phone: 270-322-0127.** (A suggested donation of $5.00 helps with postal costs.)You may also reach the ministry by e-mail at focusnews1@aol.com. An eight-page safety plan for leaving an unsafe home is available, as well as various informational brochures. Information is also available on starting a Focus support group or hosting a seminar on domestic violence.

Scriptures for Meditation

Matthew 18:2–5; 19:13–14

TWELVE

HOW TO HELP SOMEONE WHO IS BITTER

Lana was fired from a job because of poor work atten-
dance. As she left her employer's office, her parting com-
ment was, "There is no reason why I should have come
to work every day. They didn't pay me enough for that!"
This woman exhibited foolish behavior, which was
grounded in bitterness. She had not only harmed her
employer's business but herself as well.

When we feel hurt, it is easy to become bitter. Because
bitterness may appear to be justified, many people are
not aware that it is a serious problem that can have spiritual, emotional and physical consequences.

God warns us about
the effects of bitterness in
Hebrews 12:15, which
says that a bitter root can
cause torment and defile
many. Proverbs 14:30
says that the bitterness of
envy, jealousy and wrath

Can you think of someone who has wronged you or someone you love? What did he do? How did you feel toward him then? How do you feel toward him now?

183

Have you ever known someone who was bitter? What was he like? Have you ever been bitter? If so, what effects did bitterness have on you spiritually, emotionally or physically?

causes illnesses. James 3:14–16 tells us that bitterness leads to defiance, confusion and all sorts of evil practices. When we help someone reject bitterness, we are helping him heal.

A bitter person has allowed outward circumstances to determine his attitude. Some common statements that bitter people make are:

"I'll never get over this."

"I'll never forget what they did."

"I'll see them pay."

"It's just not fair!"

"This will ruin my life."

"Nothing will ever be the same because of what they did."

"It's all their fault!"

"Why is God doing this to me?"

"No matter what they do, they can never make up for this."

"They don't deserve another chance."

"If this hadn't happened, I could do such-and-such, but not now."

"I don't deserve anything. I have ruined my life."

Vows of Bitterness

People who are hurt often make vows and feel justified in maintaining them. Vows have the power to bind us to the past in ways we cannot imagine. Bitterness can cause us to sabotage our lives. We begin to live our lives in order to prove a point or to get revenge.

In addition, once we have made a vow, it is difficult to back away from it. People who love us have often invested in our bitterness, and when we want to let it go, they cannot understand. They almost feel betrayed.

Have you ever found yourself making these statements? If so, have your statements been directed more toward yourself or others? Have you ever been bitter toward God?

People who choose to remain bitter usually build a case for continuing their toxic response to harm. Comments that indicate a justification for bitterness are:

"See? I knew it! They're all alike!"
"I knew it! It happens every time!"
"This isn't the first time, and it won't be the last!"
"Nothing will ever change."
"It's always been this way and it always will be."

When you are helping people, listen for cues to bitterness. As Christians, we are admonished to "exercise foresight and be on the watch to look [after one another], to see that no one falls back from and fails to secure God's grace" (Hebrews 12:15).

Outer Circumstances, Inner Responses

The attitudes of a bitter person affect and infect many because bitterness creates self-centered, self-indulgent and irresponsible behavior. Statements that illustrate such selfishness are:

"I'm always overlooked. Why should I try?"

"Things never work out for me. I'm not going to put myself out."

"Since I didn't get *this,* I should be able to have *that.*"

A friend of mine asked me to meet with her Aunt Marie who complained of chronic aches and pains. Her physicians had not been able to find the cause of her suffering. As Aunt Marie arrived at my office, she walked slowly, as if she had the weight of the world on her shoulders. Her mouth was tight and drawn. She was only 52 years old, but she looked much older.

Do you know someone who builds a case for bitterness? How does he do this? What are his relationships like?

As we began our conversation, Aunt Marie appeared to have a hard time concentrating. At one point I asked, "Have you experienced any disappointments or difficulties in your life?" Aunt Marie immediately perked up, moved to the edge of her chair and leaned forward. Her eagerness to respond was evident.

She began, "My brother robbed me of my portion of our family inheritance. Because of what he did, I didn't get to go to college. I didn't get to find a good man and get married. It's his fault that I have no children. Because I have no degree, I have no profession. I'm so mad I could spit! And don't ask me to forgive him! I never will! Just thinking about him makes me ache all over."

Aunt Marie had just diagnosed herself!

When I asked Aunt Marie how old she was when her inheritance was stolen, she said that she was eighteen years old. She had been bitter for 34 years! Most of her adult life had been invested in carrying out previous vows and building her case. The effects had become evident in her body, mind and spirit.

Bitter Compensations

When people become bitter, they often believe that they have the right to compensate themselves for the injustices of

What other choices could Aunt Marie have considered for her life? What might her life have been like if she had refused bitterness? After she lost her fortune, how could God have provided for her? Was her brother more to blame than she was for the condition of her life?

their lives. They excuse themselves from accountability.

Years ago I worked with a woman who began to have severe financial problems. She was in charge of the petty cash at our organization. When the manager discovered that some funds were missing, he found that she had been taking money for months. At first, she had been able to pay back the money she took, but gradually she took more and more and was able to pay back less and less.

Her response to the theft? "I wouldn't be in this mess if my husband hadn't left me! I deserved some help from somewhere."

Oftentimes addictions are the result of compensations for personal harm. Bitter people believe that they are entitled to be treated differently from everyone else. They may create their own compensations through harmful or illegal methods.

Blaming God

It is not inconceivable, in this process of hurt and forgiveness, that we turn our anger toward God. When life brings hurtful circumstances, we want to understand why and how they happened. Sometimes we cannot get an answer to our questions, so we blame God for allowing the pain, even though we readily confess that God does no wrong to anyone.

After the September attacks, one man said, "Well, this is God's judgment on our country because we have turned away from Him."

Another man heard him and replied angrily, "Well, if that's so, why didn't God take your son instead of mine?"

If the person you are helping blames God for the hurt she has suffered by an offender, help her learn to make an important distinction: Pain and suffering come from Satan, who does evil continually (see 1 Peter 5:8), and from our own fallen natures. We break God's laws repeatedly. We harm one another. We make mistakes and cause accidents.

God, who is perfect love, is the one who comes to our aid and helps us recover from what Satan has done to harm us and from what we have done to harm each other. God is the one who forgives us for our sins and helps us correct our mistakes. He is the one who heals us from the sins that have been committed against us by others.

Sometimes people wonder if we should ever forgive God. He never needs our forgiveness because He never fails us, but we do need to *know* Him as He really is so that we will not doubt Him.

If your friend is bitter toward God, suggest that she read John 10:10 in which Jesus explains the source of evil. Jesus said, "The thief comes only in order that he may steal and may kill and may destroy. I came that they may have and enjoy life, and have it in abundance—to the full, till it overflows." Also point to James 1:13–14, which explains how we are enticed by our own evil desires; we are not tempted by God to sin, for He tempts no one.

Help her understand that if we do not understand God's character and blame Him for our pain, we will lose our ability to trust Him.

The Antidote for Bitterness

If your friend wants to be cleansed of bitterness, God has a cure. It is forgiveness. After having counseled with people for almost thirty years, however, I have found that few believers really understand what forgiveness means.

In one of my seminars, I asked the audience, "What does it mean to forgive?" Someone responded, "It means to forgive and forget." Another said, "You have to act as if nothing happened." Someone else said, "Forgiveness means that you let them off the hook."

With beliefs like these, it is easy to see why many people are so reluctant to forgive! Under these belief systems there is no recognition of sin, no justice and no plan for safety in the future! Because of these deceptions, many remain victims all their lives.

The Dynamics of Forgiveness

When someone does harm to another, the action according to Scripture (see Matthew 16:23) is called an *offense. Strong's Concordance* defines *offense* as "something that causes someone to stumble, to trip up or to entice to sin."

A man named James suffered an offense and fell into just that scenario: "I have been angry for months because my son's basketball coach molested him. I can't seem to let it go, even though the guy is in prison. It's crazy. . . . I think about it all the time and plan ways to

189

make him pay. Yet he can never pay enough for what he did!"

James' initial anger concerning the harm done to his son could be justified. He used his anger appropriately to press charges against the coach. However, as the months went by, he allowed himself to continue to be angry until the anger hardened into bitterness that was consuming his life and leading him into sin.

James continued, "I find myself getting angry at innocent people. It's as if I am trying to make everyone pay for what happened."

Has it been difficult for you to forgive someone? Were you waiting until justice was accomplished? Are you still trying to make someone pay?

James' anger was no longer profitable, meaning that he was no longer using the energy of the anger constructively. Instead, it had become harmful to him, as well as to those around him. It was past time for James to forgive.

When I approached the subject of forgiveness with him, James' response was typical of most people who have been offended.

He exclaimed, "Forgive him? No way! He doesn't deserve to be forgiven! It's not fair for him to spend just a few months or years in prison after what he did to my son. My son is more important than that!

James believed that unless he supplied the punishment himself, the offender would not be justly punished. Forgiving the perpetrator of his son's assault made no sense to him.

The Definition of Forgiveness

Was James right in his assessment? Let's look more closely at the subject of forgiveness.

According to *Strong's Concordance, forgiveness* means "to be merciful, to pardon, to purge away, to put off and to reconcile."

But what about justice? Is the perpetrator really to be "let off the hook"?

As James and I began to discuss his feelings, we studied Romans 12:19, which says, "Beloved, never avenge yourselves, but leave the way open for [God's] wrath; for it is written, Vengeance is Mine, I will repay (requite), says the Lord."

James thought about this for a moment. "So if I let go of my anger," he reasoned, "God will still remember. He says that He will repay. Even if the offender is put on parole, God will see that He gets the punishment he deserves in some way. God won't forget my son."

James began to see that God does not disregard the offenses against us. In fact, He offers to undertake justice *for* us, releasing us from the heavy burden of using precious moments of our lives trying to punish those who have harmed us.

Then James had this insight: "Criminal law punishes people who molest children. If even the criminal law punishes perpetrators, why would I think God would let the issue drop if justice is not complete? His promises were made to my son, as well as to me. I am going to believe God's Word. Even after I forgive the perpetrator, God will still see that justice is done."

As he continued to study God's Word, James was able to release his anger and trust God to keep His promise. As the months went by, James was free to spend time with his son, enjoying their activities together instead of wearing himself out with anger. James and his son were free to move on with their lives, no longer bound by the actions of the perpetrator.

What about Reconciliation?

We must be prepared for the fact that our forgiveness does not necessarily lead to change on the part of our offenders. The same person who caused harm before may attempt to cause harm again if given the opportunity.

Is there someone you need to forgive? Do you see this as an acceptable choice? If the relationship continues, what are some changes that you might need to require? If this person is still harmful, how can you protect yourself?

Forgiveness and relationship are separate issues. Ideally, forgiveness would result in better relationships, but this does not always happen. There may be no change in those relationships this side of heaven. In fact, even when we have forgiven someone, we may still need to protect ourselves from harm.

A Priority Reason to Forgive

If the person you are helping is struggling to forgive, ask him if he would like to be like his offender. Let me explain.

Recently I met Rhonda, a woman in her mid-fifties. When she was a child, her mother assaulted her physically and verbally. As Rhonda began to tell her story, she sobbed. "I have so many regrets," she said. "I haven't spoken to my mother since I left home more than forty years ago. And now my daughter hasn't spoken to me in the last five years. She says that she never wants to hear the sound of my voice again. No matter how hard I tried not to, I have to admit that I treated her just as my mother treated me! When she was born, I promised myself that I would never treat her that way. But I did. *How could this have happened?"*

Rhonda related several incidents of abusing her daughter, exclaiming, "I hate my mother and what she did! What I can't understand is, how could I possibly have done the same thing?"

How? I am convinced that *we become like the people we think about.* If we have been hurt and have not forgiven, the person who hurt us becomes the frequent centerpoint of our thoughts.

Rhonda was a perfect example of this. Listen to her words: "I never meant to abuse my daughter. When I got angry with her, my mother's words came back to me. I tried not to say them, but I did. I became just like her. I *became* my mother!"

Think of the person who has hurt you the most. Ask God to show you whether or not you have forgiven him or her. If you have not, ask Him to show you ways that you may be like him or her.

Most of us do not want to be like those who have hurt us. However, it seems inevitable. If we focus on those who harmed us, their words and actions will be firmly imprinted in our minds. Each time we bring their words to mind, we are unknowingly training ourselves to become like them. *We become like those we think about the most.* Even though we may resist it, a negative example is powerful. The more we think about our offenders, the more like them we become. The only way to detach from their image is to forgive them.

If you are helping someone who is serious about forgiveness, here is a list of questions you may ask.

- Have you become like your offender in any way? Have you allowed bitterness to affect your character? Do you want to be this way?

- Do you still play out mentally a scenario of revenge or justice? Are you willing to trust God to be your Avenger? Will you release the injustices of your life into His hands?
- Have you continued to blame him or her for what he or she did? Have you let your bitterness influence your decisions in life? What has your bitterness cost you?

Do you have traits that are similar to those of someone who has harmed you? If you do, ask yourself the above questions.

- If something good happened to him or her, could you be glad?
- Would you like to have peace? Would you like to shed the tight skin of bitterness and become the person God designed you to be?

An Exercise for Forgiveness

Sometimes when we are ready to forgive our offenders, we need to get practical. Offer your hurting friend this exercise.

Ask him to get a legal pad and write the name of his offender at the top of the page. Then ask him to make three columns.

In the first column, record each offense. (This may be abbreviated or written in code.) In the second column, ask him to write the approximate date on which the offense was committed against him. In the third column, record the amount of time that has passed since the offense occurred. Continue until all offenses are listed.

When the lists are complete, ask him to total the amount of time in the last column. That number will serve as an indicator of how many years of bitterness your friend is carrying.

I worked with a nineteen-year-old young woman who had been molested by her brother and two uncles. Because of what had happened, she experienced constant fear and withdrew from other children as she was growing up. During her teenage years, she never went on a date because she felt soiled. I met her soon after she was released from the hospital with heart disease. When she completed the above exercise, she found that she had been carrying more than 2,500 years of bitterness in her body!

When your friend has completed the assignment, and it may take some time before all offenses have been recalled and recorded, ask him to bring the list and meet with you. Then ask him to join you in prayer. As you pray, invite your friend to offer the list to Jesus. Read Hebrews 10:21–23, emphasizing that Jesus is his High Priest, able to understand and sympathize with him. Ask Jesus to be the Avenger. Bow before Him and place the list of offenses in His hands. Invite your friend to release all bitterness, trusting Jesus to avenge him.

When the offenses are released, pray for cleansing and healing for your bitter friend. Pray for the Holy Spirit to come and begin a new work.

If your friend blames himself in any way, ask him to insert his own name in the exercise and follow the same process.

Nancy's Story

I close here with a story by a woman named Nancy. May her example be an inspiration to you and the one you are helping.

When my mother died after a two-year battle with ovarian cancer, I lost a major source of unconditional love. She had been my champion, friend and mentor. I had never been very close to my father. After my mother's death I began getting to know him for the first time.

After a full year of solitude and meals-for-one at his kitchen table, my father was ready to live again. He asked my sister and me for permission to date the church pianist. We were fine with the idea.

In just a few months, Daddy was "in love." My sisters found it amusing to see him behaving like a junior-high boy with a crush. While on a visit to my home, he asked me to take him to a card shop so he could purchase a stockpile of "meaningful" cards to send to "her."

As I watched my father experiencing a love I had never seen him have with my mother, a seed of bitterness began to grow.

My father married the pianist and I had never seen him so happy. A few weeks after their marriage, I received a birthday card that said, "To a Wonderful Daughter." It was lovely except for the fact that he had signed his name and *her* name on it. I was offended that he could replace Mother so easily. In my anger, I planned to bring up this topic during our next phone call and ask him never to do that again. During the week, I practiced my little speech, full of indignation and hurt.

On the morning of my father's regular call, the Holy Spirit spoke to my heart: *Can you simply be happy for the love and joy your father has found after such sorrow? You mother is in heaven now, free and peaceful. She is not holding on to any of this, so why are you?* As I heard His voice, I was able to release my anger and, instead, enjoy a pleasant phone chat with my father.

Ten days later I got a call informing me that my father had died from an aneurysm. The sorrow and shock were surreal. But in the midst of the chaos, I could thank God for restraining me that morning. The Holy Spirit had warned me and made it possible for me to have delightful memories of our last conversation instead of bitter rancor and regrets.

Realizing my orphaned state, I claimed the promise of Psalm 27:10: "Although my father and my mother have forsaken me, yet the Lord will take me up [. . . as His child]."

With your encouragement, your friend may come to realize that we do not always have time left in which to forgive and to save ourselves from bitterness.

Scriptures for Meditation

Matthew 18:21–35
Ephesians 4:31–32
Philippians 3:13–14
Colossians 3:13
Hebrews 10:30
1 Peter 2:19–23; 3:9–12

THIRTEEN

How to Help Someone Who Is Fearful

Peace I leave with you; My [own] peace I now give and bequeath to you. Not as the world gives do I give to you. Do not let your heart be troubled, neither let it be afraid—stop allowing yourselves to be agitated and disturbed; and do not permit yourselves to be fearful and intimidated and cowardly and unsettled.

John 14:27

In the summer of 1990, experts predicted that an earthquake would occur on a specific day in December along the New Madrid fault line, which lies in southeastern Arkansas and southern Missouri. Wayne had just begun a new job only twenty miles from the fault line, and each week he traveled along the fault line from our house to the town in Missouri where he was working.

As we waited for our house to sell, I paid little attention to the media's doomsday prediction. Some reports said that the earthquake could kill thousands of people, including residents of several surrounding states. As time passed, their descriptions of disaster became more and more graphic. They predicted that buildings and bridges would crumble. There would be power failures and extensive flooding along the banks of the Mississippi River. I remained calm and detached from their words for several weeks.

My peace began to waver, though, as I continued to listen to the reactions of people around me. Imaginations were beginning to flourish. Neighbors were buying earthquake insurance and stocking up on water, food and other supplies. Communities were having earthquake drills. People were storing their valuables. Schools were declaring disaster holidays, and many people were making plans to leave the area entirely.

Finally, I began to allow myself to form mental pictures of these disasters, including potential harm to Wayne. Would he be driving along the fault line when the earthquake hit? What if he happened to be crossing a bridge when it collapsed? What if the tremors caused him to have a wreck?

Once I allowed fear to begin, it grew rapidly and I expressed my fear to Wayne. My husband is a highly responsible, duty-bound man, and he gave no credence to my anxiety. When I asked him weeks ahead not to travel on the day of the predicted quake, he looked at me as if I had suggested the most ridiculous thing in the world! He continued to go about his life unperturbed, even though his new company was planning for rescue efforts and buying flashlights and bottled water. They even bought body bags!

As Wayne became more and more determined to fulfill his duty by showing up for work as usual, I became even more fearful. How could I make him see that he might really be in danger? Our lives could be changed forever in one day. We had a chance to prevent harm, and he was not willing to hear me! I felt helpless to do or say anything that gave me peace. I was living Proverbs 12:25, which says that anxiety in the heart weighs it down. My heart was heavy and I was exhausted from *carrying all that fear around.*

Finally, I accepted the fact that Wayne was determined to place himself on the fault line of the impending earthquake! Knowing there was nothing more I could say or do, I had to give up. I accepted the fact that only God can control the future. Only God could protect Wayne, so I began an earnest search for faith.

When you have been fearful for a long period, what effect did the fear have on your mind and body?

I wrote Psalm 91 and Psalm 121 in my journal and began to memorize them. I said them aloud as I drove to work each day. The power of God's Word began to sustain me, and the fear began to fade away.

Two weeks before the predicted earthquake, I drove up the fault line to visit Wayne. As I passed the exit signs for various small towns, I prayed for the safety and well-being of the people who lived there. When I arrived in the town where Wayne was working, I drove up and down the streets, praying for the people who lived in each house. I recited Psalm 91 and Psalm 121 aloud as I drove past the stores downtown. I prayed for rescue workers, physicians and hospital personnel. As I prayed, my confidence increased.

When I returned home, I took another step toward faith as I read 1 Peter 5:6–7:

Therefore humble yourselves (demote, lower yourselves in your own estimation) under the mighty hand of God, that in due time He may exalt you. Casting the whole of your care—all your anxieties, all your worries, all your concerns, once and for all—on Him; for He cares for you affectionately, and cares about you watchfully.

> *Can you relate an experience when God replaced your fear with peace? Were you able to cast your care? If so, how did you do it?*

I knew that it was past time for me to cast my cares on Him about the earthquake, but I did not know what a care was and I did not know what it meant to cast it on Him. What was I supposed to do?

As I continued my search, I found that a *care* is the burden of negative emotions that overshadow us when trouble comes. *Cares* are a composite of doubt, fear and dread.

I decided to list every specific issue that came to mind, including Wayne's safety, the effect on our family if a catastrophe actually occurred, plus my fear of his death. I prayed that God would deliver me from all my cares.

Then I made an altar on the hearth of our fireplace, using a lighted candle, my Bible, pictures of our family and a cross. I read the list of cares out loud to God and dropped it into the fire. As the fire consumed the symbol of my fear, I offered myself to God for His use, asking that my mind be kept in perfect peace. I was given the ability to entrust Wayne to God.

On "the day of the earthquake," I went to work as usual, giving thanks to God for watching over us all. I did not think of the earthquake again until mid-afternoon! God had exchanged the fear for peace as He has promised in Isaiah 26:3–4:

> You will guard him and keep him in perfect and constant peace whose mind [both its inclination and char-

acter] is stayed on You, because he commits himself to You, leans on You and hopes confidently in You. So trust in the Lord—commit yourself to Him, lean on Him, hope confidently in Him—for ever; for the Lord God is an everlasting rock—the Rock of ages.

Just as Wayne predicted, the earthquake did not occur. My fears were for nothing. Rescue helicopters were canceled, body bags were stored and water and food supplies were gradually used throughout the next year. All was well.

Why Do Believers Worry?

I opened this chapter with Jesus' beautiful words of assurance. As believers we know the truth of these words. We know that His peace is available to us and that He does not want us to fall into the snare of worry. Since we have such strong reassurance from Jesus about fear, why do Christians still fear so much?

Can you give examples of situations in life that frighten you or those you love? Have those situations already occurred or are they worries about the future?

Here are a number of reasons. See if the person you are helping identifies with them.

We are deceived.

Today Sandra is a strong woman, full of faith. However, she learned to worry early in life believing the lie that it was the only way she could handle her fears. Looking back, she said, "Even as a child, I lived under a cloud of fear. Everything frightened me! As a young adult, I was filled with fear. When I married, I carried fear into my marriage. My husband did not respect me because I was afraid to speak up. He began to control me. I lived in a grown-up body, but inside, I was still a fearful child and I acted like one. I found myself in a prison with walls so thick and bars so tight that I could not escape. It is almost impossible for fearful people to grow up because we do not even realize that we are afraid. Fear becomes a way of life."

Satan is the author of fear (see 2 Timothy 1:7) and he does not hesitate to afflict small children. Like Sandra, many are imprisoned in fear and do not even realize it, but God offers hope and release.

Does worry really show that we care? Was someone in your family the queen or king of worry? Did it make you feel loved to know that someone was losing sleep because of circumstances in your life? Would you have preferred for him or her to use that energy to pray for you, or to say simply, "I love you"?

Sandra continued, "When I was almost forty, I met a friend who began to straighten the bars of my twisted grid with truth. I learned quickly, however, that I couldn't just change my way of thinking overnight. It would take time and work, but I was so desperate for help that the possibilities seemed like a miracle to my hurting soul. I have done my work with God. I have come a long, long way from the frightened, fear-filled woman that I once was. My heart sings with freedom and joy!"

We are trained to worry.

Many of us have been taught to worry. A client told me, "My mother was the *queen* of worriers and she taught me well. She would say, 'I'm supposed to worry about you! It's my job! If I don't worry about you, who will? There's no telling what would happen to you if I didn't worry!'"

We want members of our family to know that we love them, so we assure them that we worry about them. When we do this, we make worry a noble virtue and teach our children to pass fear down to the next generation.

Worry makes us feel as if we are accomplishing something.

Once a man said to me, "Well, I couldn't think of anything to do about my circumstances, so I thought the least I could do was to worry about them! At least I feel as though I'm doing *something!*"

He was doing something, all right! He was wasting his energy in a non-productive manner. When the time came that there might be something he could actually *do,* he would probably be too tired to do it.

One worry can distract us from another.

Janis was a woman with long-term marriage problems. I could always tell when the difficulties had intensified. Instead of talking about her marriage, she would begin our session by saying, "I'm so worried about my weight! I've gained two pounds this month."

Do you have a favorite worry? If so, what do you use it to avoid? What have been the effects of your "escape"?

When she felt fearful and helpless in her marriage, it was less painful to worry about her weight. After all, she could do something about that!

Often when people become extremely fearful, they will detach their emotions from one area of life and attach them to one less fearful. If this action is carried to an extreme, obsessions can begin.

For example, after Melanie recovered from injuries she sustained during a serious car wreck, she was afraid to drive. When it became absolutely necessary for her to drive again, she would get into her car, become fearful, get out and go into her house to make sure she had turned off the stove. Over a period of time, her fears escalated. She began to think of other things to "check on" before she cranked up her car. She exclaimed, "I check the stove, the iron, the washer, the dryer and the lights! Sometimes I drive away and make myself go home and check again and again."

People who become trapped in obsessions or compulsions need professional help.

Solutions for Those Who Worry

Worry and fear are not the answers to our problems. If your friend has trouble in this area, offer the following helps.

Cast your cares.

It is helpful to perform outwardly the inner action of casting a care. When we become tempted to fear, the memory of the ceremony will come to mind and help sustain our faith.

A simple way to help someone cast a care is to make a worry box. Suggest that the fearful person get a strong cardboard box. Ask her to write down her worries. Then ask her to write portions of God's Word at the bottom of the list, ending with a written prayer asking God to take all the cares and worries. Next, take string and tie the box with many, many knots. Have her put the box in a place where she will see it often. Ask her to make this agreement: If she decides she simply *must* worry, she will untie every knot, take out the paper and worry intensely for at least thirty minutes. Then she will tie the box again and recast her cares.

A friend of mine named Connie was the mother of a seventeen-year-old wayward daughter. Her daughter seldom attended her classes at school. She had begun to drink and smoke marijuana. When her daughter was ticketed for driving while intoxicated and taken to jail, Connie was distraught! She had taught her daughter well, disciplined her, listened to her, talked with her and set firm limits, but her daughter's misbehavior only escalated. Connie slept very little during those months.

She agreed to make a worry box. She wrote down her fears and various Scriptures about God's peace. Then she wrote a prayer that included every area of her daughter's life for at least the next ten years! She prayed about her safety, her college education, her future husband, her work and the children she might have some day.

Do you know someone who trades a severe fear for a lesser fear? Do you know someone who is bound by obsessions or some type of compulsive behavior? If so, do you know of professionals in your area who could be helpful?

She then placed her list of fears, the Scriptures and her prayer in a beautiful gold box. She took a purple ribbon and tied it in knots all around the box. Finally, she placed the box on the cedar chest at the foot of her bed. Each time she found herself being tempted to carry heavy emotions, she knelt beside the cedar chest and thanked God that He had heard all of her prayers, and she once again became established in peace.

Surrender absolutely.

The most productive thing you can encourage someone to do when she is faced with fear is to surrender all that she is and has to Jesus. Surrender is difficult for some people because they are afraid of God.

Do you need to make a worry box? Do you have a specific fear?

This happened to a man named Tom. When he was ten years old, his father died. When he asked where his father was, a well-meaning uncle explained, "Well, Tom, God needed your dad more in heaven than we need him here, so He took him away to heaven. He's with God now."

From that moment on Tom saw God as someone who would swoop down at any moment and take away someone he loved. As an adult, he remained alert, ready to protect himself and his loved ones from God. Tom was a chronic worrier. He could not trust God.

If you are helping someone who does not trust God, suggest a study on God's love and peace. Look at the life of Jesus and do a character study. Some verses you may review are:

Isaiah 9:6; 26:3
John 14:27
Romans 5:1
Galatians 5:22–23
Colossians 3:15

Recognize that worry is a sin.

If you are helping a fearful believer, encourage her to confess her fear and worry as sin. Admonish her to turn against it.

Jenny, a chronic worrier, said, "When I realized that worry really is sinful, I began to respond to the temptation to worry just as I would respond to the temptation to commit other sins. When I began to feel the pull toward worry, I would resist it just as I would resist stealing from a department store. I simply ceased to condone worry."

Watch out for the lies connected with worry.

Fear and worry belong to the evil one. The Bible says that Satan is the father of lies. When he speaks fear to us, he is not speaking truth.

For instance, one of Satan's most common lies is, "Don't try. You'll fail." On the contrary, if God has called you to do something, you can do it! Fear is the opposite of faith, and when we choose to believe the lies of fear, we are placing our faith in Satan and his evil outcome.

Accept the reality of inadequacy.

One of the most common statements I hear is, "I feel so inadequate." It is normal to feel nervous about accepting a new challenge. That does not mean, however, that we cannot do what we are called to do. Encourage yourself and others to take action *while* you are afraid. The fear will soon fall away.

St. Paul experienced fear, but he did not allow it to stop him. In 1 Corinthians 2:3, he said, "I (passed into a state of) weakness and was in fear (dread) and great trembling [after I had come] among you." Verse 4 informs us that, in spite of his fear, Paul spoke in such power that the minds of the listeners were stirred and persuaded to believe.

Encourage action.

As I mentioned earlier, although we may feel fearful we can continue with our lives. It may be helpful to encourage people to take small steps. Help them break down big tasks into small tasks.

For example, Lloyd was afraid to fly after the attacks of September 11. This fear was a severe handicap for him because he was required to travel to other states in his work. His first step was to educate himself regarding new safety measures that were being put into place. His second step was to choose an airline that had an excellent safety record and book a short flight on his day off. His third step was to consider several ways in which he might protect himself if a terrorist appeared on his plane in the future. The night before his first flight, Lloyd armed himself with prayers about God's presence. His last step was to go to the airport and board the plane, entrusting his fears to God. After that first short flight, Lloyd was able to approach his regular work flights without extreme anxiety.

Have you ever done something that you were terribly afraid to do? How did you feel after you accomplished your task? Can you encourage someone else with your victory?

Teach worriers to curb their imaginations.

People who worry usually have active, vivid imaginations.

I have a friend named Anne who is very creative. She paints, decorates and sews. She can imagine a beautiful scene and put it onto a canvas, or walk into a dismal environment and make it delightful. When she becomes frightened, though, she can also "design" an imaginary disaster.

When you are helping a fearful person, give her a symbol that will enable her to curb her imagination. When Anne found herself imagining catastrophes, usually at night, she visualized her fearful thoughts as a small spiral in her brain that increased in size as it was allowed to grow. She kept a pair of large scissors by her bed. Whenever she sensed the spiral starting to spin, she took the scissors and "cut off" the spiral at its base. Anne reported, "Having a visual method of stopping the worry is so helpful to me. It stops my imagination immediately."

Share this exercise with your fearful friend and ask if she would be willing to participate in it for thirty days, which is the least amount of time it takes to break a habit.

Professional Help

If the person you are helping continues to be fearful, suggest getting professional assistance. Symptoms that consistently plague those who need professional help are:

Feeling restless, keyed-up or often on edge
Fatigue
Muscle tension
Heart palpitations
Sleep disturbances, nightmares
Hypervigilence (constantly alert to danger)
Obsessive/compulsive behaviors
Resistance to medication

Sandra told me the conclusion of her story of finding freedom from fear. "After years of enduring frowns and criticism from my family and acquaintances about my fear, I found a physician who suggested medication. I was elated to find myself experiencing relief! As the medication assisted me in controlling my anxiety, I could focus much more easily on the recovery work God had placed before me."

Fear does not have to stop before we act. As we begin to face fear, courage comes and faith takes over.

Shannon's Story

Shannon suffered for years because she let fear rule her life. Here is her story of finding freedom.

I have always been fearful. I have been afraid to fly in planes, ride buses or take elevators, and I have experienced constant fear that I would die and leave my children without a mother. I understood how my fears started, and I knew that they were extremely exaggerated, but I couldn't help myself.

When my daughters became teenagers, I was forced to face my fear of flying. They wanted to participate in a dance contest, and it was in a distant state. Just the thought of flying made me nauseous. I began to have severe muscle tension in my neck and back. I did not see how I could make myself get on the plane when the time came. I sought help from several believers who prayed for my mental state, as well as our safety on the flight.

After they prayed for me, my anxiety dropped to a low level. When it was time to board the plane, I was pretty calm, expecting a smooth flight. When we had been in the air for a while, however, the pilot announced that we would soon experience severe turbulence. The plane began to toss up and down and side to side. When we were supposed to land, the landing gear was lowered and then raised again eight times. People around me were crying and holding onto each other. Two people near me vomited.

I cried out to God and said, "I can't believe You would let the thing I fear the most happen to me! I trusted You when I got on this plane. I know that perfect love casts out fear, but I don't feel loved by You because You're letting this flight be so scary! I feel betrayed!"

Then I heard God's voice speak to me. It wasn't actually audible, but I heard Him. He said, *You will walk through the fire, but you will not be burned.* Suddenly I was overcome with a sense of His presence, love and peace. I still wasn't sure that we would live, but I knew that even though I was going through a fiery trial, I would come out unscathed either on earth or in heaven.

Ten minutes later, we landed safely. I threw my hands into the air and cried, "Hallelujah!" God had let me face my greatest fear while flying—the fear that I would die—and had showed Himself faithful in the middle of it!

God delivered me of the fear of flying. I am planning another trip in two months.

I am God's beloved child, and now I know that from my own experience. He will never abandon me. He will come when I need Him most.

God is faithful. Even though we are afraid, we can trust Him to carry us through. Your friend can be set free from the bondage of fear and move into the security of Jesus' perfect peace. It begins by moving ahead, believing that He will guide step-by-step.

Scriptures for Meditation

Psalms 31:24; 56:11; 91:4–7
Isaiah 54:14
John 14:27
Romans 8:5, 29, 31, 35–39
Hebrews 13:6

FOURTEEN

THE IMPORTANCE OF CELEBRATING ACHIEVEMENTS

Recently I taught a workshop at a music seminar in Atlanta presented by Babbie Mason, a Christian songwriter and singer. Each year, Babbie and her husband, Charles, provide a marvelous opportunity for aspiring songwriters and singers to get the information and training they need to pursue their dreams.

The atmosphere was almost electric as participants readied their presentations for the competition near the end of the week. The winner would be awarded several prizes, including some travel trips with Babbie to various conferences. Every participant wanted to win.

When the last night came, and the winners were to be announced, anticipation was high! Those who had participated could hardly breathe as they waited to hear the results. When the scores were announced, the winners came forward and received their awards. The audience stood and applauded. Cameras were clicking on all sides. The cheers were deafening. Then they performed their winning songs. There was more applause, more cheers and standing ovations. That was a moment none of the winners would ever forget. Their hard work, dedication, persistence and patience had paid off.

It is possible that the victories of those you have helped will not be as recognizable as those of the contest winners. There are no score cards or high water marks to measure. Nevertheless, it is always appropriate to recognize people for their victories. In fact, you may be the only one in their "audience" who knows or notices what they have done. The people you help will be strengthened by your recognition of their successes, no matter how small or insignificant they may seem.

Last year I worked with a woman who had to start her life over. Her husband had left her. Because she dropped out of high school to marry him, she never had a job that would pay her enough to live on. She had not developed her abilities through education or job training. She felt helpless.

This woman started with a part-time job. She took night classes and got her GED. Then she began taking computer training. Her pursuits required a sacrifice of time and money. She had to form new study habits so that she could pass the tests. Her schedule seldom allowed time for leisurely activities. With all the various adjustments she had to make, it was difficult for her to be consistent in her efforts. Because she was still grieving over the death of her marriage, it was hard for her to concentrate and keep her focus, but she never gave up.

When she completed the computer classes, her friends gave a celebration dinner for her. When she applied for her first full-time job, they prayed for her and cheered her onward.

When she got the job, they had flowers delivered on her first day at work!

I am sure you are probably thinking, *Now that's what friends are for!* If you are thinking that, you are exactly right.

Celebrations are mile-markers for our progress. When we achieve something significant, whether in a professional or personal arena, we need to celebrate.

I lead growth groups that last four to six weeks each fall and spring. Each participant sets goals at the beginning of our sessions. At the end of the sixth week, I bring helium-filled balloons and marking pens to the meeting. Each person is instructed to write on the balloon words of thanksgiving for the progress she has made and a request for the future. After each person has completed her task, we go outside, sing a praise song, release the balloons and watch our many-colored "praises" and requests rise toward heaven.

> *Has anyone ever held a celebration in your honor? If so, how did you feel? Have you ever accomplished something significant and found yourself all alone? Was there no one to celebrate with you? If so, what was that like?*

> *If you sent up a balloon today, what praise would you have to offer? What has God done in your life? Do you have a request you would like to send?*

As one member of the group watched the balloons rise, she commented, "Oh, just *look* how many prayers God answered!" Concrete displays of progress and praise leave a distinct impression.

Remember that every celebration is twofold: 1) to glorify God and show thanksgiving for what He has done and 2) to recognize what a person can do as he or she allows God to empower him or her. It is a celebration of that partnership and the results of it.

Recognizing Your Friend's Milestones

Since our successes are not usually as obvious or significant as those of a contest winner, we need to make up our minds to watch for them. What would it have been like if the participants in the contest had practiced and performed and won, but no one had noticed? After every trial, there should be a reward. You can have the joy of giving it!

People remember those little kindnesses. They tell other people about them. They replay the memories over and over in their minds. Recognition causes people to thrive. It makes them want to continue.

Can you recall small steps that someone took? What were they? Did you celebrate? If not, how might it have helped?

When you first begin working with someone, make a mental note of his goals. There will be larger goals that will include smaller, step-by-step goals along the way. Remember to watch for the steps.

Someone once told me, "You are one of the few people I know who build celebration points into ministry." That surprised me because when we work with Jesus, there *is going to be* reason to celebrate. He is going to hear our prayers, help us and move us forward step-by-step. As long as the person you are helping has the desire to succeed, there will be many reasons to celebrate. Keep your eyes open!

The celebration does not have to be elaborate. Here are some of the simple ways I have seen people rejoice with others for their accomplishments:

218

Send a flower

Take a picture

Make a poster

Send a card

Get tickets to a special event

Give a new Bible or book and add a thoughtful inscription

Get a blue ribbon

Send up a balloon

Give a magnet or refrigerator art

Go out for donuts

Go out for a meal

Buy a small trophy and have it engraved

Go to a movie

Buy bubble bath

Treat to a massage

Symbols of victories always create strength. They confirm this important truth: "You can do it! You did do it! And you can do it again!"

My husband is a marathon runner. The runners are awarded trophies and T-shirts at the end of races. Wayne's souvenir marathon posters are all over our house. I had his medals framed, and they are displayed in our living room. Just the sight of those posters and medals is inspiring. They remind him of what is possible. From time to time, we talk about them and remember his victories.

Celebrations for *You!*

Because you have also persevered and invested in the victory, God has rewards for you. Our God is one who celebrates! Remember that after He delivered the Israelites from Egypt and led them into the Promised Land, He inaugurated a calendar of Feasts. Several of them were festivals of joy and rejoicing over their deliverance (see Exodus 23:14). Others were celebrations of thanksgiving and joy for the Lord's blessing of the harvest (see Leviticus 23:40). We celebrate the birth of Jesus. We are baptized in celebration of the death of our old lives and entry into our new lives. At Easter, we celebrate the Resurrection. There are many types of symbols to illustrate what has occurred, such as bread and wine, crosses, banners and songs that we sing.

Can you think of additional ways to celebrate? Is there someone you can celebrate with today?

The grand and final celebration will be at the Marriage Supper of the Lamb. If you are in Christ, you will be invited. Revelation 19:7–9 says:

> Let us rejoice—and shout for joy—exulting and triumphant! Let us celebrate and ascribe to Him glory and honor, for the marriage of the Lamb [at last] has come and His bride has prepared herself.

No matter how large or small your contribution may have been to your friend in your own eyes, God has seen it.

Even good deeds done in secret are seen by God. Matthew 6:4 tells us that when we give gifts in secret, our Father who sees secret things will reward us *openly*.

This year I worked with a woman who was willing to recognize that she had become self-centered and selfish. In order to become more aware of the needs of those around her, she agreed to do one secret act of kindness each day. She prayed about the deed that she would do each morning, and before the day was over she had quietly done what God had instructed her to do.

As the days passed by, she exclaimed, "It truly is more blessed to give than to receive! I know the Lord is with me as I reach out to the people around me. I feel His hand of blessing on me. I have felt His love as I have never felt it before. And because my giving is strictly between Him and me, I feel closer to Him than ever before."

When her time for rewards comes, those secret kindnesses will be brought out into the open and there will be even more rewards.

My Prayer for You

I pray that as you reach out to people who need you, you will be filled with the power of the Holy Spirit. I pray that you will be given the ears to hear His voice and the will to obey as He gives you insight and instruction. Above all I pray that you experience His presence, His joy and most of all His love for you and those you serve. May you be blessed in your earthly labor and rewarded greatly in heaven.

Lynda D. Elliott, a member of the American Association of Christian Counselors, has been helping people for more than twenty-five years. The author of several books, including *An Invitation to Healing,* she has been an adjunct professor for Trinity College and Seminary and teaches nationally and internationally. A personal life coach living in Little Rock, Arkansas, Lynda is a frequent conference speaker who also provides seminars for lay counselors and church leaders.

If you are interested in having Lynda Elliott speak at a conference or workshop, you may reach her by calling (501) 224-5015 or by checking out her web site at <www.lyndadelliott.com>.

Also by LYNDA ELLIOTT

AN INVITATION TO HEALING
Let God Touch Your Mind, Body and Spirit

Do you—or someone you love—need emotional, spiritual or physical help?

If your body is carrying the weight of hurtful emotions like depression, shame, regret or fear, this remarkable book on healing is for you. Most of us pray and hope that healing will just "happen," but healing is a process. What does God do and what does He want us to do? This book will bring you closer to our Lord Jesus Christ and prepare you for the process.

Praise for AN INVITATION TO HEALING

"Lynda Elliott is one in a million. She goes straight to the heart. She doesn't push and she doesn't twist words. Her book on healing is a safe, simple, personal invitation. Decide for yourself."
—**Jan Silvious,** author, broadcaster, counselor

"An important book. Clergy and lay people will find valuable insights in this balanced book about healing."
—**Lyle W. Dorsett, Ph.D.,** Wheaton College

"This book can increase your knowledge and build your faith. These insights offer hope for hurting hearts."
—**Nancy Grisham,** Billy Graham Center Institute of Evangelism

"A must-read. Everyone has been hurt in life. I recommend these valuable insights for everyone."
—**Susan Walker,** Willow Creek Association

"Elliott's experience and wisdom are awesome! I will use this book in my classes."
—Pamela C. Peterson, Ph.D., Trinity College and Seminary

"Invaluable to those who serve on prayer teams and to those who are hurting."
—**Linda Strom,** author, *Karla Faye Tucker—Set Free*